Bloom's BioCritiques

Dante Alighieri
Maya Angelou
Jane Austen
James Baldwin
William Blake
Jorge Luis Borges
The Brontë Sisters
Lord Byron
Geoffrey Chaucer
Anton Chekhov
Joseph Conrad
Stephen Crane
Charles Dickens
Emily Dickinson
William Faulkner
F. Scott Fitzgerald
Robert Frost
Ernest Hemingway
Langston Hughes
Zora Neale Hurston
Franz Kafka
Stephen King
Gabriel García Márquez
Herman Melville
Arthur Miller
John Milton
Toni Morrison
Edgar Allan Poe
J.D. Salinger
William Shakespeare
John Steinbeck
Henry David Thoreau
Mark Twain
Alice Walker
Eudora Welty
Walt Whitman
Tennessee Williams

Bloom's BioCritiques

Gabriel García Márquez

Edited and with an introduction by
Harold Bloom
Sterling Professor of the Humanities
Yale University

CHELSEA HOUSE
P U B L I S H E R S
A Haights Cross Communications Company ®
Philadelphia

©2006 by Chelsea House Publishers, a subsidiary of
Haights Cross Communications.

A Haights Cross Communications ➤ Company ®

www.chelseahouse.com

Introduction © 2006 by Harold Bloom.

Printed and bound in the United States of America.

10 9 8 7 6 5 4 3 2 1

Library of Congress Cataloging-in-Publication Data
Bloom, Harold.
  Gabriel García Márquez / Harold Bloom.
      p. cm. — (Bloom's biocritiques)
  Includes bibliographical references and index.
  ISBN 0-7910-8115-X
  1. García Márquez, Gabriel, 1928- I. Title. II. Series.
  PQ8180.17.A73Z598 2005
  863'.64—dc22
                                          2005008632

Contributing editor: Grace Kim
Cover design by Keith Trego
Cover: © Getty Images, Inc.
Layout by EJB Publishing Services

CONTENTS

USER'S GUIDE

These volumes are designed to introduce the reader to the life and work of the world's literary masters. Each volume begins with Harold Bloom's essay "The Work in the Writer" and a volume-specific introduction also written by Professor Bloom. Following these unique introductions is an engaging biography that discusses the major life events and important literary accomplishments of the author under consideration.

Furthermore, each volume includes an original critique that not only traces the themes, symbols, and ideas apparent in the author's works, but strives to put those works into a cultural and historical perspective. In addition to the original critique is a brief selection of significant critical essays previously published on the author and his or her works followed by a concise and informative chronology of the writer's life. Finally, each volume concludes with a bibliography of the writer's works, a list of additional readings, and an index of important themes and ideas.

HAROLD BLOOM

The Work in the Writer

Literary biography found its masterpiece in James Boswell's *Life of Samuel Johnson*. Boswell, when he treated Johnson's writings, implicitly commented upon Johnson as found in his work, even as in the great critic's life. Modern instances of literary biography, such as Richard Ellmann's lives of W.B. Yeats, James Joyce, and Oscar Wilde, essentially follow in Boswell's pattern.

That the writer somehow is in the work, we need not doubt, though with William Shakespeare, writer-of-writers, we almost always need to rely upon pure surmise. The exquisite rancidities of the Problem Plays or Dark Comedies seem to express an extraordinary estrangement of Shakespeare from himself. When we read or attend *Troilus and Cressida* and *Measure for Measure*, we may be startled by particular speeches of Ulysses in the first play, or of Vincentio in the second. These speeches, of Ulysses upon hierarchy or upon time, or of Duke Vincentio upon death, are too strong either for their contexts or for the characters of their speakers. The same phenomenon occurs with Parolles, the military impostor of *All's Well That Ends Well*. Utterly disgraced, he nevertheless affirms: "Simply the thing I am / Shall make me live."

In Shakespeare, more even than in his peers, Dante and Cervantes, meaning always starts itself again through excess or overflow. The strongest of Shakespeare's creatures—Falstaff, Hamlet, Iago, Lear, Cleopatra—have an exuberance that is fiercer than their plays can contain. If Ben Jonson was at all correct in his complaint that "Shakespeare wanted art," it could have been only in a sense that he may not have intended. Where do the personalities of Falstaff or Hamlet touch a limit? What was it in Shakespeare that made *Hamlet* and the two parts of *Henry IV* into "plays unlimited"? Neither Falstaff nor Hamlet will be stopped: their wit, their beautiful, laughing speech, their intensity of being—all these are virtually infinite.

In what ways do Falstaff and Hamlet manifest the writer in the work? Evidently, we can never know, or know enough to answer with any authority. But what would happen if we reversed the question, and asked: How did the work form the writer, Shakespeare?

Of Shakespeare's inwardness, his biography tells us nothing. And yet, to an astonishing extent, Shakespeare created our inwardness. At the least, we can speculate that Shakespeare so lived his life as to conceal the depths of his nature, particularly as he rather prematurely aged. We do not have Shakespeare on Shakespeare, as any good reader of the Sonnets comes to realize: they do not constitute a key that unlocks his heart. No sequence of sonnets could be less confessional or more powerfully detached from the poet's self.

The German poet and universal genius, Goethe, affords a superb contrast to Shakespeare. Of Goethe's life, we know more than everything; I wonder sometimes if we know as much about Napoleon or Freud or any other human being who ever has lived, as we know about Goethe. Everywhere, we can find Goethe in his work, so much so that Goethe seems to crowd the writing out, just as Byron and Oscar Wilde seem to usurp their own literary accomplishments. Goethe, cunning beyond measure, nevertheless invested a rival exuberance in his greatest works that could match his personal charisma. The sublime out-rageousness of the Second Part of *Faust*, or of the greater lyric and meditative poems, forms a Counter-Sublime to Goethe's own daemonic intensity.

Goethe was fascinated by the daemonic in himself; we can doubt that Shakespeare had any such interests. Evidently, Shakespeare abandoned his acting career just before he composed *Measure for Measure* and *Othello*. I surmise that the egregious interventions by Vincentio and Iago displace the actor's energies into a new kind of mischief-making, a fresh opening to a subtler playwriting-within-the-play.

But what had opened Shakespeare to this new awareness? The answer is the work in the writer, *Hamlet* in Shakespeare. One can go further: it was not so much the play, *Hamlet*, as the character Hamlet, who changed Shakespeare's art forever.

Hamlet's personality is so large and varied that it rivals Goethe's own. Ironically Goethe's Faust, his Hamlet, has no personality at all, and is as colorless as Shakespeare himself seems to have chosen to be. Yet nothing could be more colorful than the Second Part of *Faust*, which is peopled by an astonishing array of monsters, grotesque devils and classical ghosts.

A contrast between Shakespeare and Goethe demonstrates that in each—but in very different ways—we can better find the work in the person, than we can discover that banal entity, the person in the work. Goethe to many of his contemporaries seemed to be a mortal god. Shakespeare, so far as we know, seemed an affable, rather ordinary fellow, who aged early and became somewhat withdrawn. Yet Faust, though Mephistopheles battles for his soul, is hardly worth the trouble unless you take him as an idea and not as a person. Hamlet is nearly every-idea-in-one, but he is precisely a personality and a person.

Would Hamlet be so astonishingly persuasive if his father's ghost did not haunt him? Falstaff is more alive than Prince Hal, who says that the devil haunts him in the shape of an old fat man. Three years before composing the final *Hamlet*, Shakespeare invented Falstaff, who then never ceased to haunt his creator. Falstaff and Hamlet may be said to best represent the work in the writer, because their influence upon Shakespeare was prodigious. W.H. Auden accurately observed that Falstaff possesses infinite energy: never tired, never bored, and absolutely both witty and happy until Hal's rejection destroys him. Hamlet too has infinite energy, but in him it is more curse than blessing.

Falstaff and Hamlet can be said to occupy the roles in Shakespeare's invented world that Sancho Panza and Don Quixote possess in Cervantes's. Shakespeare's plays from 1610 on (starting with *Twelfth Night*) are thus analogous to the Second Part of Cervantes's epic novel. Sancho and the Don overtly jostle Cervantes for authorship in the Second Part, even as Cervantes battles against the impostor who has pirated a continuation of his work. As a dramatist, Shakespeare manifests the work in the writer more indirectly. Falstaff's prose genius is revived in the scapegoating of Malvolio by Maria and Sir Toby Belch, while Falstaff's darker insights are developed by Feste's melancholic wit. Hamlet's intellectual resourcefulness, already deadly, becomes poisonous in Iago and in Edmund. Yet we have not crossed into the deeper abysses of the work in the writer in later Shakespeare.

No fictive character, before or since, is Falstaff's equal in self-trust. Sir John, whose delight in himself is contagious, has total confidence both in his self-awareness and in the resources of his language. Hamlet, whose self is as strong, and whose language is as copious, nevertheless distrusts both the self and language. Later Shakespeare is, as it were, much under the influence both of Falstaff and of Hamlet, but they tug him in opposite directions. Shakespeare's own copiousness of language is well-nigh incredible: a vocabulary in excess of twenty-one thousand words, almost eighteen hundred of which he coined himself. And of his word-hoard, nearly half are used only once each, as though the perfect setting for each had been found, and need not be repeated. Love for language and faith in language are Falstaffian attributes. Hamlet will darken both that love and that faith in Shakespeare, and perhaps the Sonnets can best be read as Falstaff and Hamlet counterpointing against one another.

Can we surmise how aware Shakespeare was of Falstaff and Hamlet, once they had played themselves into existence? *Henry IV, Part I* appeared in six quarto editions during Shakespeare's lifetime; *Hamlet* possibly had four. Falstaff and Hamlet were played again and again at the Globe, but Shakespeare knew also that they were being read, and he must have had contact with some of those readers. What would it have been like to discuss Falstaff or Hamlet with one of their early readers (presumably also part of their audience at the Globe), if you were the creator of such demiurges? The question would seem nonsensical to most Shakespeare scholars, but then these days they tend to be either ideologues or moldy figs. How can we recover the uncanniness of Falstaff and of Hamlet, when they now have become so familiar?

A writer's influence upon himself is an unexplored problem in criticism, but such an influence is never free from anxieties. The biocritical problem (which this series attempts to explore) can be divided into two areas, difficult to disengage fully. Accomplished works affect the author's life, and also affect her subsequent writings. It is simpler for me to surmise the effect of *Mrs. Dalloway* and *To the Lighthouse* upon Woolf's late *Between the Acts*, than it is to relate Clarissa Dalloway's suicide and Lily Briscoe's capable endurance in art to the tragic death and complex life of Virginia Woolf.

There are writers whose lives were so vivid that they seem sometimes to obscure the literary achievement: Byron, Wilde, Malraux, Hemingway. But most major Western writers do not live that exuberantly, and the greatest of all, Shakespeare, sometimes appears to have adopted the personal mask of colorlessness. And yet there are heroes of literature who struggled titanically with their own eras— Tolstoy, Milton, Victor Hugo—who nevertheless matter more for their works than their lives.

There are great figures—Emily Dickinson, Wallace Stevens, Willa Cather—who seem to have had so little of the full intensity of life when compared to the vitality of their work, that we might almost speak of the work in the work, rather than even of the work in a person. Emily Brontë might well be the extreme instance of such a visionary, surpassing William Blake in that one regard.

I conclude this general introduction to a series of literary bio-critiques by stating a tentative formula or principle for gauging the many ways in which the work influences the person and her subsequent, later work. Our influence upon ourselves is always related to the Shakespearean invention of self-overhearing, which I have written about in several other contexts. Life, as well as poetry and prose, is overheard rather than simply heard. The writer listens to herself as though she were somebody else, and the will to change begins to operate. The forces that live in us include the prior work we have done, and the dreams and waking visions that evade our dismissals.

HAROLD BLOOM

Introduction

I

Macondo, according to Carlos Fuentes, "begins to proliferate with the richness of a Columbian Yoknapatawpha." Faulkner, crossed by Kafka, is the literary origins of Gabriel García Márquez. So pervasive is the Faulknerian influence that at times one hears Joyce and Conrad, Faulkner's masters, echoed in García Márquez, yet almost always as mediated by Faulkner. The *Autumn of the Patriarch* may be too pervaded by Faulkner, but *One Hundred Years of Solitude* absorbs Faulkner, as it does all other influences, into a phantasmagoria so powerful and self-consistent that the reader never questions the authority of García Márquez. Perhaps, as Reinard Argas suggested, Faulkner is replaced by Carpentier and Kafka by Borges in *One Hundred Years of Solitude*, so that the imagination of García Márquez domesticates itself within its own language. Macondo, visionary realm, is an Indian and Hispanic act of consciousness, very remote from Oxford, Mississippi, and from the Jewish cemetery in Prague. In his subsequent work, García Márquez went back to Faulkner and Kafka, but then *One Hundred Years of Solitude* is a miracle and could only happen once, if only because it is less a novel than it is a Scripture, the Bible of Macondo; Melquíades the Magus, who writes in Sanskrit, may be more a mask for Borges than for the author himself, and yet the Gypsy storyteller also connects García Márquez to the archaic Hebrew storyteller, the Yahwist, at once the greatest of realists and the greatest of fantasists but above all the only true rival of Homer and Tolstoy as a storyteller.

My primary impression, in the act of rereading *One Hundred Years of Solitude*, is a kind of aesthetic battle fatigue, since every page is rammed full of life beyond the capacity of any single reader to absorb. Whether the impacted quality of this novel's texture is finally a virtue I am not sure, since sometimes I feel like a man invited to dinner who has been served nothing but an enormous platter of Turkish Delight. Yet it is all story, where everything conceivable and inconceivable is happening at once, from creation to apocalypse, birth to death. Roberto González Echevarría has gone so far as to surmise that in some sense it is the reader who must die at the end of the story, and perhaps it is the sheer richness of the text that serves to destroy us. Joyce half-seriously envisioned an ideal reader cursed with insomnia who would spend her life in unpacking *Finnegans Wake*. The reader need not translate *One Hundred Years of Solitude*, a novel that deserves its popularity as it has no surface difficulties whatsoever. And yet, a new dimension is added to reading by this book. Its ideal reader has to be like its most memorable personage, the sublimely outrageous Colonel Aureliano Buendía, who "had wept in his mother's womb and been born with his eyes open." There are no wasted sentences, no mere transitions, in this novel, and you must notice everything at the moment you read it. It will all cohere, at least as myth and metaphor if not always as literary meaning.

In the presence of an extraordinary actuality, consciousness takes the place of imagination. That Emersonian maxim is Wallace Stevens's and is worthy of the visionary of *Notes toward a Supreme Fiction* and *An Ordinary Evening in New Haven*. Macondo is a supreme fiction, and there are no ordinary evenings within its boundaries. Satire, even parody, and most fantasy—these are now scarcely possible in the United States. How can you satirize Ronald Reagan or Jerry Falwell? Pynchon's *The Crying of Lot 49* ceases to seem fantasy whenever I visit Southern California, and a ride on the New York City subway tends to reduce all literary realism to an idealizing projection. Some aspects of Latin American existence transcend even the inventions of García Márquez. I am informed, on good authority, that the older of the Duvalier dictators of Haiti, the illustrious Papa Doc, commanded that all black dogs in his nation be destroyed when he came to believe that a principal enemy had transformed himself into a black dog. Much that is fantastic in *One Hundred Years of Solitude* would be fantastic anywhere, but much that seems unlikely to a North American critic may well be a representation of reality.

Emir Monegal emphasized that García Márquez's masterwork was unique among Latin American novels, being radically different from the diverse achievements of Julio Cortázar, Carlos Fuentes, Lezama Lima, Mario Vargas Llosa, Miguel Angel Asturias, Manuel Puig, Guillermo Cabrera Infante, and so many more. The affinities to Borges and to Carpentier were noted by Monegal as by Arenas, but Monegal's dialectical point seemed to be that García Márquez was representative only by joining all his colleagues in not being representative. Yet it is now true that, for most North American readers, *One Hundred Years of Solitude* comes first to mind when they think of the Hispanic novel in America. Alejo Carpentier's *Explosion in a Cathedral* may be an even stronger book, but only Borges has dominated the North American literary imagination as García Márquez has with his grand fantasy. It is inevitable that we are fated to identify *One Hundred Years of Solitude* with an entire culture, almost as though it were a new *Don Quixote*, which it most definitely is not. Comparisons to Balzac and even to Faulkner are also not very fair to García Márquez. The titanic inventiveness of Balzac dwarfs the later visionary, and nothing even in Macondo is as much a negative Sublime as the fearsome quest of the Bundrens in *As I Lay Dying*. *One Hundred Years of Solitude* is more of the stature of Nabokov's *Pale Fire* and Pynchon's *Gravity's Rainbow*, latecomers' fantasies, strong inheritors of waning traditions.

Whatever its limitations may or may not be, García Márquez's major narrative now enjoys canonical status as well as a representative function. Its cultural status continues to be enhanced, and it would be foolish to quarrel with so large a phenomenon. I wish to address myself only to the question of how seriously, as readers, we need to receive the book's scriptural aspect. The novel's third sentence is: "The world was so recent that things lacked names, and in order to indicate them it was necessary to point," and the third sentence from the end is long and beautiful:

> Macondo was already a fearful whirlwind of dust and rubble being spun about by the wrath of the biblical hurricane when Aureliano skipped eleven pages so as not to lose time with facts he knew only too well, and he began to decipher the instant that he was living, deciphering it as he lived it,

prophesying himself in the act of deciphering the last page of
the parchment, as if he were looking into a speaking mirror.

The time span between this Genesis and this Apocalypse is six
generations, so that José Arcadio Buendía, the line's founder, is the
grandfather of the last Aureliano's grandfather. The grandfather of
Dante's grandfather, the crusader Cassaguida, tells his descendant Dante
that the poet perceives the truth because he gazes into that mirror in
which the great and small of this life, before they think, behold their
thought. Aureliano, at the end, reads the Sanskrit parchment of the
gypsy, Borges-like Magus, and looks into a speaking mirror, beholding
his thought before he thinks it. But does he, like Dante, behold the
truth? Was Florence, like Macondo, a city of mirrors (or mirages) in
contrast to the realities of the Inferno, the Purgatorio, the Paradiso? Is
One Hundred Years of Solitude only a speaking mirror? Or does it contain,
somehow within it, an Inferno, a Purgatorio, a Paradiso?

Only the experience and disciplined reflections of a great many
more strong readers will serve to answer those questions with any
conclusiveness. The final eminence of *One Hundred Years of Solitude* for
now remains undecided. What is clear to the book's contemporaries is
that García Márquez has given contemporary culture, in North America
and Europe, as much as in Latin America, one of its double handful of
necessary narratives, without which we will understand neither one
another nor our own selves.

II

The aesthetic principle of *Love in the Time of Cholera* is only a
slightly chastened version of what might be the motto of *One Hundred
Years of Solitude*: "Anything goes", or even "Everything goes". Anything
and everything goes into the mix: Faulkner, Kafka Borges, Carpentier,
Conrad, Joyce. Both novels are Scriptures: *Solitude* is an Old Testament,
and *Cholera* a New Testament, at least for García Márquez and the most
devoted of his readers and critics. I myself have come to value *Cholera*
over *Solitude*, but that is a choice of riches.

What Faulkner—who most valued the Bible (as literature only),
Shakespeare, Melville, Conrad, and Joyce—would have made of these
New World Hispanic masterpieces, I cannot surmise. The verbal
cascades he would have recognized as akin to his own, and the heroic

individualism surely would have moved him. Yet he went about while waiting for his doom to lift, and his greatest figures—Darl Bundren, Quentin Compson, Sutpen, Joe Christmas, Popeye—are damned beyond damnation. Though Faulkner could be as grandly comic as Dickens, as is witnessed by the Snopes family, who now constitute the Texan Republican party, led by Tom De Lay Snopes, while our nation has chosen Benito Bush as Il Duce. Oscar Wilde was always right: life has no choice but to imitate art.

The antic joy of García Márquez might have been shrugged away by Faulkner, at least in his tragic mode, but he would have approved the last-ditch humanism affirmed both by precursor and latecomer. Decadence, the obsessive fear of incest, the drowning out of creative solitude by an ocean of information: these are common themes and apprehensions. What then is the saving difference, besides amazing high spirits in García Márquez, that distinguishes the two?

Faulkner's hopes rarely are persuasive: his greatest characters are as nihilistic as Shakespeare's. The immense popularity of García Márquez was earned by his exuberance, which veils his own apocalyptic forebodings. What Shakespeare was to Faulkner, Cervantes necessarily is to García Márquez: the truest ancestor. Cervantes, in his dark wisdom, is not less nihilistic than Shakespeare, and I do not believe that either ultimately was a Christian believer, any more than Faulkner or García Márquez can be said to be.

García Márquez's difference from all three is more evident in *Cholera* than in *Solitude*: he really does have a High Romantic faith in Eros, though he knows the Freudian truth that love too frequently is a mask for the Death Drive. Yet I prefer *Cholera* to *Solitude* finally because Florentine Ariza is dauntless, as here in the novel's closing passage:

> "Let us keep going, going, going, back to La Dorada."
>
> Fermina Daza shuddered because she recognized his former voice, illuminated by the grace of the Holy Spirit, and she looked at the Captain: he was their destiny. But the Captain did not see her because he was stupefied by Florentino Ariza's tremendous powers of inspiration.
>
> "Do you mean what you say?" he asked.
>
> "From the moment I was born," said Florentino Ariza, "I have never said anything I did not mean."
>
> The Captain looked at Fermina Daza and saw on her

eyelashes the first glimmer of wintry frost. Then he looked at Florentino Ariza, his invincible power, his intrepid love, and he was overwhelmed by the belated suspicion that it is life, more than death, that has no limit.

"And how long do you think we can keep up this goddamn coming and going?" he asked.

Florentino Ariza had kept his answer ready for fifty-three years, seven months, and eleven days and nights.

"Forever," he said.

AMY SICKELS

Biography of Gabriel García Márquez

Finding the Magic in the Everyday

After a terrible massacre in the town, it rains for four years, eleven months, and two days. A beautiful woman draped in sheets ascends to heaven. A priest drinks a cup of chocolate, then levitates six inches off the ground. An entire town forgets the names of even the most basic objects. The sky rains yellow flowers.

These are just a few of the astounding and memorable images that appear in Gabriel García Márquez's masterpiece *One Hundred Years of Solitude*. Critics have praised the work as "biblical" in its scope, an epic that has delighted readers across the world, taking them through one hundred years of the lives of the Buendía family.

Initially influenced by experimental Latin American writers such as Jorge Luis Borges and Alejo Carpentier, and American authors William Faulkner and Ernest Hemingway, García Márquez eventually found his own voice and style. He is often credited as the master of magical realism, the literary technique in which no distinction is made between reality and the fantastic. However, the unique voice found in his work did not appear as soon as he began writing—it was something he struggled to discover. Although he had written four books before *One Hundred Years of Solitude*, it was not until his furious writing of this novel that he fully discovered his voice, a voice which he claims was that of his grandmother.

García Márquez grew up in the 1930s in his grandparents' house

1

in a coastal town rich with legends and myths. Aracataca, recognized as the "banana town," was known to its inhabitants for its violent downpours and thick, sultry heat. Bitter-almond trees with magnificent green leaves stood along the yards of the traditional multi-colored plank houses with high-peaked tin roofs. Sometimes a traveling circus would come through town, and García Márquez's grandfather would take him to watch.

The drafty, large house where he grew up seemed to hold as many secrets, scares, and delights as the town itself. As a child, García Márquez often felt frightened in the large roomy house, where his grandmother said ghosts walked the halls. It was she who taught him at an early age that the real and the supernatural, the living and the dead, overlapped. She belonged to a world of myth, magic, and superstition, and it was not unusual for her to talk to the dead. Once, she told him not to comb his hair at night because it would cause a ship to be lost at sea. As a child, he was curious about an electrician who would come to the house, wearing a belt he used to suspend himself from the electrical posts. His grandmother told him every time this man came around, he would leave the house full of butterflies. Later, when García Márquez began writing fiction, he realized the way to make these fantastic stories believable was to be specific. For example, he claimed that if he did not say the butterflies were yellow, no one would believe the scene. In *One Hundred Years of Solitude*, García Márquez masters this mix of exaggeration and specificity.

García Márquez has often said that in Latin America, magical realism is perfectly ordinary—that the strangest, oddest things happen every day—and he repudiates fantasy writing. He once explained, "Fantasy, in the sense of pure and simple Walt-Disney-style invention without any basis in reality is the most loathsome thing of all ... The difference between [imagination] and [fantasy] is the same as between a human being and a ventriloquist's dummy" (*Guava* 31). He also admits, however, that the imagination beckons one to leave the ground and to explore a fictional world. The critic Stephen Minta summarizes: "The problem for a writer in Latin America, García Márquez has often observed, lies not in finding a subject, but in ensuring credibility, in making the reader understand that the sense of wonder and infinite strangeness which emerges from much Latin American writing is a true reflection of the complex realties of Latin American experience, not merely the product of a feverish, literary imagination" (37). García Márquez manages to convey this by blending exaggeration and specificity, and by creating a magical, believable world such as that of Macondo, the setting of *One Hundred Years*.

Although Aracataca, his childhood home, held many nostalgic memories for him, García Márquez did not know that he wanted to write about this place until he made a painful, bittersweet journey back to Aracataca when he was twenty-two years old. His grandmother had died, and he went back with his mother to sell the family house. He soon discovered that the town and his grandparents' house were not the way he had remembered them.

Now he saw Aracataca through the eyes of an adult; he saw it as a hot, sleepy, poor, and shabby town in which his grandparents' house had also dilapidated. His grandfather had died years ago, and his grandmother, her eyesight nearly gone, spent her last days muttering with the dead and allowed the house to fall into shambles. The almond trees had been eaten by ants, and the garden's plants and flowers had shriveled and died.

García Márquez described the return trip in an interview:

When I got there it was at first quite shocking because I was now twenty-two and hadn't been there since the age of eight. Nothing had really changed, but I felt that I wasn't really looking at the village, but I was experiencing it as if it were reading it. It was as if everything I saw had already been written, and all I had to do was to sit down and copy what was already there and what I was just reading. For all practical purpose everything had evolved into literature: the houses, the people, and the memories. (Stone 321)

The return trip symbolized the end of his childhood, yet also provoked his rich memories of the place. The critic Stephen Minta explains:

For García Márquez, the return to Aracataca was deeply disturbing, and provided a strong impulse to locate the nature of that disturbance in writing. The loss of his childhood home, and the sense of the terrible circularity

which was returning Aracataca to the nothingness from
which it had come, both contributed to the desire to create,
however deceptively, the story of that house and of that
community in a work of fiction. (46)

After he left Aracataca, he began writing a narrative called "La
casa" inspired by his grandparents' house. As Minta further notes, his
grandparents' house came to symbolize "the private, familial
representation of the larger process of disintegration which carries
Aracataca, or Macondo, out of history and back into the endless cycle of
mythological time" (34).

However, at the time, he was too young and inexperienced as a
writer to create this epic narrative. Instead, the story would be turning
in him for another fifteen years. Though bits and pieces slipped out in
stories, Macondo and the story of the Buendías would not be fully born
until the day he sat down to begin writing *One Hundred Years of Solitude*.
Yet on that emotional day when he returned to his grandparents' empty
house, the twenty-two year old García Márquez discovered his calling to
be a writer.

CHILDHOOD: MYTHS AND LEGENDS

Gabriel José García Márquez was born on March 6, 1927 to Gabriel
Eligio García and Luisa Santiaga Márquez Iguarán, in Aracataca,
Colombia. Though the actual year of his birth has been disputed—for
most of his life critics and García Márquez himself have cited his birth
as 1928—García Márquez recently attested that he believes the earlier
year is correct. He was the first born of twelve children (he had a total
of fifteen siblings, including four elder siblings who were the children of
other women, born before his father married his mother). For the first
part of his life, García Márquez was raised as an only child. Until he was
eight years old, García Márquez lived with his maternal grandparents in
the small coastal town, Aracataca.

During this time, it was not uncommon in the Caribbean for
grandparents to raise a child whose parents were struggling to make ends
meet. It was also likely that García Márquez's parents "gave" him to his
grandparents, in part, out of conciliation, as his grandparents had been
strongly opposed to his parents' marriage.

García Márquez's mother descended from a higher-standing social class than his father, and for several reasons, her parents staunchly opposed the marriage. One reason concerned Gabriel Eligio's status as an outsider. Gabriel Eligio had spent several years studying medicine at the University of Cartagena, on the Caribbean coast, but had dropped out of school because of lack of money. He arrived to work as a telegraph operator in Aracataca in the 1920s, after the "banana fever" had made the town prosperous. As the critic Stephen Minta observes, "The well established families of Aracataca, of which García Márquez's grandparents were one of the most eminent representatives, inevitably looked with disfavor on the invasion of fortune-seeking outsiders" (37).

García Márquez's grandfather also opposed his daughter's romance with Gabriel Eligio because he was born illegitimately, and was rumored to have been with many different women. At one point, García Márquez's grandfather attempted to break up the relationship by sending Luisa off to stay with relatives and possibly playing a hand in arranging for Gabriel Eligio to be transferred to work in another town. However, while they were separated, Gabriel Eligio sent Luisa love messages by wire, and their romance blossomed. He also seduced her with poetry, violin serenades, and letters. Eventually, García Márquez's grandfather accepted Gabriel Eligio as his son-in-law.

Perhaps most alarming for García Márquez's grandfather, who identified as a steadfast Liberal, was that his son-in-law Gabriel Eligio called himself a Conservative. In a country that possesses, like most Latin American countries, a complicated, exhausting history of civil wars, dictators, *coups d'etat*, and social revolutions, politics have always played an important role. Two main parties, the Conservatives and the Liberals, have dominated the political scene for many years. García Márquez's grandfather, Colonel Nicolás Márquez, fought in the Thousand Days' War of 1899–1902, in which he was a colonel in the Liberal ranks. He served under the well-known Liberal General Rafael Uribe Uribe. The bloody, violent Thousand Days' War resulted from a culmination of civil conflicts—over sixty civil wars were fought between 1820 and 1903. The Thousand Days' War claimed at least one hundred thousand lives, though the actual number was probably closer to 300,000.

The two central political parties, the Conservatives and Liberals, were at one time clearly separated by both location and ideology. The Conservatives, strongest in the river valleys and mountains, favored a centralized government, limited suffrage, and a strong church; whereas the Liberals, maintaining a stronghold in the coastal zones, supported more tolerance and secularization, more individual rights, and greater federalism. During the twentieth century, the two factions often overlapped in their politics, yet people remained fiercely loyal to their chosen, or "inherited," party. Affiliation sometimes resulted more from family loyalty than ideology. A popular saying among Colombians has been "being a Conservative or Liberal depends on what your father is" (*Guava* 96). In the case of García Márquez, although his father was a Conservative, he was raised as a Liberal by his grandfather. Though he identified early on as a Liberal, García Márquez has also dismissed both groups as being part of a corrupt ruling oligarchy, claiming that his political views are independent of both parties.

Geographically, Columbia spans almost twice the size of Texas, with a population of over forty million. Its diverse geographical areas differ radically from each other, in both environment and culture. For instance, the chilly Andean mountains contrast with the humid Amazon. Whereas the Caribbean shore, in the north, is characterized by tropical heat, the ocean, and aromas of seafood, the capital of Colombia, Bogotá, is located high in the Andes Mountains in the central part of the country. Four hundred miles of jungle and mountains separate the two areas, their differences not only geographical but also cultural. Citizens of the coast, known as *costeños*, or "coastals," describe their attitudes as more laid-back and their speech more informal than in Bogotá. *Costeños* listen to salsa music and participate in drumming circles, and maintain a powerful sense of loyalty and pride in their mix of African, indigenous Indian, and Hispanic roots.

Gabriel García Márquez spent the first eight years of his life barely knowing his parents and living with his grandparents in this environment. The town of Aracataca and his grandparents formed his earliest memories, and influenced his beliefs and personality. He has claimed that he learned everything that was important in life during this period.

Aracataca, a small, dusty town on the coast, later turned into the magical, doomed town of Macondo that appears in much of García Márquez's fiction. It was a land where the weather varied from sultry, tropical heat to wild, torrential downpours. Although Aracataca currently boasts a population of 20,000, it was not nearly this large when

García Márquez lived there. In an area once known as the banana zone, Aracataca lies to the south of the capital of the Magdalena department, Santa Marta, on the railway line that connects the capital with the interior. The town was founded around the end of the nineteenth century by people fleeing the civil wars. One of these settlers was García Márquez's grandfather who moved to Aracataca after the Thousand Days' War and played a hand in turning the town into a Liberal stronghold.

Aracataca was also the sight of the infamous Banana Strike Massacre in 1928, which occurred a year after García Márquez was born. At the end of the nineteenth century, during the "banana fever," the U.S. corporation, the United Fruit Company (now Chiquita Brands International), had expanded into Aracataca. With its arrival, the town seemed ripe for prosperity and wealth, and many outsiders, such as García Márquez's father, arrived to seek their fortune. The company built private swimming pools and cultivated green lawns for its corporate leaders, while the migrant workers they brought with them lived in poverty-stricken homes. The company also constructed and maintained its own railroad, irrigation network, telegraph network, and retail stores, and created fenced-in residential compounds so that the North Americans could maintain their own social life apart from the locals. The U.S. company avoided required labor practices, such as providing workers with medical care and sanitary conditions, and used a scrip system in which workers were paid in scrip redeemable only at company stores conveniently stocked with expensive goods from the United States. In 1928, the United Fruit Company's harsh labor practices finally incited 32,000 field workers to go on strike. When the trouble began brewing, the company claimed that no employees were on its payroll and burned the evidence of employment cards and poof of eligibility for pensions. In retaliation, the strikers stopped trains, damaged cut fruit, and blocked scabs, and the fruit company called in the Colombian army. When the strikers assembled at the Ciénaga train station, located just a few miles from Aracataca, to hold a demonstration, the troops opened fire. Under quiet consent of the United Fruit Company, the army murdered hundreds of workers, though the exact number is under debate. The Colombian government quickly suppressed information about the massacre.

By the time García Márquez was a child, the town's economic

property, and its tragedies, had slipped into the past. Aracataca had already seen its only period of economic boom come and go, and was now grappling with poverty and abandonment. "When he was born the 'banana fever' had subsided, and a community that had, until recently, been alive, vigorous, and apparently prosperous, was now returning to the timeless insularity from which it had been so unexpectedly drawn," adds Minta (34). The influences of colonialism left its heavy imprints upon the town, as in, for example, the wire fences guarding the luxury houses, revealing the harsh contrast between the area's wealth and dire poverty.

The history of the town's violence, coupled with the beautiful setting, would later appear in much of García Márquez's fiction. In fact, a few miles from Aracataca lay a banana plantation called "Macondo"— the name of the mythical town in *One Hundred Years of Solitude*.

Although Aracataca provided the young García Márquez— nicknamed "Gabito" as a child, which later became "Gabo"—with historical and mythical material, it was the influence of his grandparents, with their fabulous stories and legends, that truly colored his imagination. He lived with his grandparents in a large, roomy house, the smell of jasmine ripe in the air. As influential people in the town, Gabito's grandparents attracted a large number of guests. Furthermore, his grandfather, Nicolás Márquez, had fathered over a dozen illegitimate children, and often cousins, nephews, grandchildren, and other kin, dropped by. García Márquez's many aunts and his grandmother ran the household, and the unique habits and stories of the women later found their way into García Márquez's fiction. For example, one of his aunts wove her own shroud, and when Gabito asked why, she simply said, "Because I'm going to die, child," and true to her word, when she had completed the shroud, she lay down and died (*Guava* 12).

Gabito's grandfather, Nicolás Márquez, liked to reminisce about his participation the Thousand Days' War. He spoke of the battles, sieges, and the dying men. Haunted by the act of killing a man, he would often say to his grandson, "You can't imagine how much a dead man weighs" (*Guava* 13). Nicolás Márquez was "an old-fashioned, small-town gentleman who liked fine lotions, carried a pocket watch with a thick gold chain, and always wore a suit and tie" (Bell-Villada, 43). He took García Márquez to the circus and cinema, and to the United Fruit Corporation stores to show him the magical invention of ice. They often stood on the edges of the private resort-like neighborhoods that had been built for the corporate executives, observing the glistening blue swimming pools. García Márquez has claimed that his grandfather was the person in his life that he missed the most—that he was "the person I've gotten on with the best in my life and with whom I've had the best understanding" (*Guava* 18). Though, as the critic Regina Janes points out, his grandfather was "almost certainly the origin of his grandson's interest in battered old men" (10), only one of his many old men characters was based on his grandfather—the nameless colonel in *Leaf Storm*.

García Márquez established a close relationship with his grandfather that no other adult could match; however, he was not the only person to influence García Márquez. It was the voice of his grandmother, Tranquilina Iguarán, that actually emerged in his fiction. Tranquilina loved to tell stories. She believed in ghosts and talked about people without distinguishing between the dead and the living. She relayed messages in her dreams with a matter-of-fact attitude and told the young García Márquez many myths and supernatural stories, which delighted and frightened the young boy. He believed at night, ghosts wandered the magical house, and later said the feeling had stayed with him well into adulthood: "During the day my grandmother's world fascinated me—I was absorbed in it, it was my world. But at night it terrified me. Even now, when I'm asleep alone in a strange hotel in some part of the world, I often wake up in a panic, shaken by this terrible fear of being alone in the dark, and it always takes me several minutes to calm down and to go back to sleep" (*Guava* 18).

Between the violent war memories of his grandfather, and the fabulous tales of his grandmother, García Márquez learned the art and power of storytelling at a young age.

Before he knew how to write, García Márquez drew comic strips that illustrated his grandmother's fantastic stories. Once when a journalist asked García Márquez about his prose style and voice, he answered, "It's my grandmother's" (Vargas Llosa 7). His grandparents assumed opposite roles—while his grandmother believed in ghosts, his grandfather put his faith in reality—and both of their attitudes influenced García Márquez: "The strange thing was that I wanted to be like my grandfather—realistic, brave, safe—but I could not resist the constant peep into my grandmother's territory" (*Guava* 17). This combination of his grandmother's communication with the dead and the supernatural, and his grandfather's curiosity in the life around him, sparked García Márquez's rich imagination. Thus, the coastal town and his grandparents' unique personalities influenced García Márquez's early childhood years, and years later, he would base his most celebrated works of fiction on this time.

LEAVING THE COAST

When Gabito was eight years old, his grandfather died, marking the end of his magical time in Aracataca. García Márquez once claimed, "Since then nothing interesting has happened to me" (Vargas Llosa 8).

Gabito was sent to live with his parents in Sucre, a river port town. He barely knew his parents—he had not met his own mother until he was five or six years old—or any of his many siblings. He did not stay with his family for very long; soon, he was sent off to boarding school in Barranquilla, a city also on the coast, and then transferred to a school, located in the same area, that was run by Jesuits.

As a child, García Márquez was a slim, small boy with wide, alert eyes. He did not play sports, and acted so serious and somber that his classmates nicknamed him "the Old Man" (Bell-Villada 45). He was shy, curious, bright, and creative. By the age of ten, he had started composing humorous poems. When he was thirteen, he won a scholarship to attend the boarding school, Liceo Nacional de Zipaquirá, a high school for the gifted located about thirty miles outside of Bogotá.

Leaving the coast was a terrible shock for Gabito, who was accustomed to the people and the warm climate of the Caribbean coast. In the nation's capital, near his new home, the skies were gray and the weather was chilly and damp. The inhabitants also seemed different— everyone wore black, and they acted more reserved and distant than the people he had grown up around. García Márquez also remembered seeing mostly men in the city because at that time women were not allowed in many public areas. In contrast to the warmth and liveliness of the coast, everything seemed repressive and somber.

Despite his initial reaction, García Márquez adjusted to his new surroundings and received a stimulating education in politics and literature. His young teachers introduced him to Marxist thought, and social and economic history, awakening in him the first stirrings of his passion for politics. He was well-read and studious and focused on his future. The introduction he received to socialist theory and history helped shape his political convictions, and the education kindled a desire to one day be a writer. "When I left that icy prison I'd no idea where north and south were but I did have two very strong convictions," he claimed. "One was that good novels must be a poetic transposition of reality, and the other was that mankind's immediate future lay in socialism" (*Guava* 96).

After he graduated high school in 1946, García Márquez returned briefly to live with his family. Under pressure from his parents, he left in 1947 to study law at the Universidad Nacional in Bogotá. A mediocre student, García Márquez spent most of his time reading novels instead of studying. He expressed far more interest in studying literature than law. He knew that he did not want to pursue a career in law and fell into a melancholy state. The critic Gene Bell-Villada describes the student: "Floating about in a state of chronic personal depression, he led a life confined in the main to the lecture halls, the boarding house, and the nearby cafés, where, book in hand, he would show up unshaven and badly dressed" (46). Though he rarely had money as a student, he did not work to support himself, but spent his free time reading. He often went to El Molino in hopes of eavesdropping on the older, established poets and writers who frequented this café.

He read as much as he could, including the work of Jorge Luis Borges, D.H. Lawrence, Graham Greene, and Katherine Mansfield. He also attempted to read James Joyce's *Ulysses*. However, the difficulty of the book frustrated him, and he read it in bits and pieces. It was not until years later that he returned to the novel, "reading it again in a serious way, and it not only resulted in the discovery of a genuine world that I have never suspected inside me but also provided me with invaluable technical help in freeing language and handling time and structure in my own books" (*New Yorker* 102). Although García Márquez was familiar with Joyce, the Irish author was not one of his early influences, despite such claims by several critics.

One of the most significant influences on his decision to become a writer was reading Franz Kafka's "Metamorphosis." García Márquez stated that Kafka "made me want to write" (Guibert 326). In a *Paris Review* interview in 1981, he told Peter Stone that the first line of the story, about Gregor Samsa awaking as a cockroach, "almost knocked me off the bed I was so surprised ... When I read the line I thought to myself that I didn't know anyone was allowed to write things like that. If I had known, I would have started writing a long time ago" (319). After he read the story, the next day "found [him] at the portable typewriter ... trying to write something that would resemble Kafka's tale" (*New Yorker* 102). That day he wrote furiously and skipped all of his classes, fearing "the spell would be broken" (*New Yorker* 102).

He was further encouraged to continue writing fiction when Eduardo Zalamea Borda, the well-known literary editor of the Bogotá newspaper, *El Espectador*, ran an essay accusing the younger generation of Colombian writers of lacking talent. García Márquez returned to the Kafkaesque story he had started "in an attempt to prove him wrong" (*New Yorker* 102). The story, "La tercera resignación" ("The Third Resignation"), concerned a boy who had been presumed dead for eighteen years. He lay in his coffin unable to move but fully capable of thoughts and imagination. García Márquez submitted the surreal tale, and to his surprise, it appeared the following Sunday in the literary supplement, complete with a note of introduction by Zalamea Borda praising the nineteen-year-old García Márquez as "the new genius of Colombian letters" (qtd. in Mellen 13). He added that in García Márquez "a new and notable writer has been born" (*New Yorker* 104).

García Márquez, so poor at the time that he did not have the five centavos on him to buy the paper, asked a man getting out of a cab if he could have his copy. As he quickly read his short-story, he experienced the shocking effect of seeing something he had written in print: "In each line I discovered the crushing power of print, for what I had constructed with so much love and pain as a humble imitation of a universal genius was revealed to me as an obscure, weak monologue, barely sustained by three or four consolatory sentences. Almost twenty years went by before I dare to read it a second time, and my judgment then—untempered by compassion—was even less indulgent" (*New Yorker* 102). He later characterized these early stories as "intellectual stories," inspired by, but falling short of, the work of Kafka (Stone 320).

A close college friend warned García Márquez that now he would have to live up to this literary reputation he had started for himself. When García Márquez argued that his story was not well-written, his friend replied, "In any case, that story already belongs to the past... What matters now is the next one" (*New Yorker* 103). So García Márquez stayed up all night making notes for his next story. He continued to barely slide by in school, now spending all of his time at a borrowed typewriter, composing stories. His friends began to call him Maestro and introduced him to others as a writer. In the next six years, he would publish around a dozen stories in *El Espectador*.

LITERARY APPRENTICESHIP

García Márquez's law studies were interrupted on April 9, 1948, the day that Jorge Eliécer Gaitán, a Liberal leader, was assassinated. Gaitán, one of the more outspoken Liberal politicians, had caused controversy for inquiring into the banana strike and massacre of 1928. The single gunman who shot him was then attacked by an angry mob. Bogotá exploded with riots—fires were started, windows broken, and churches trashed. At least 2,000 people were reportedly killed in the riots. Though García Márquez escaped unharmed, the boardinghouse where he was staying burned to the ground, and he lost many of his books and manuscripts. The university closed down because of the riots, and García Márquez transferred to Universidad de Cartagena, located on the coast.

The assassination of Gaitán and the riots that followed set off years of violence, and this period, from approximately 1948–1958, became known as *la violencia* (the violence). Informal civil wars and armed conflicts broke out between Liberals and Conservatives, and for nearly a decade, violence continued from all groups, including the army, police, guerrillas, and gangsters. The country nearly fell into a state of anarchy. Violence erupted in the rural countryside and within the government offices. In 1949, President Mariano Pérez Ospina ordered Liberal departmental governors ousted, and that same year, Conservative House members actually drew revolvers and killed a Liberal congressman on the floor. In 1950, the Conservative Laureano Gomez took power and unleashed another war of repression against the Liberals. The opposition resisted with equaled ferocity, torching villages and murdering Conservatives. Over the years, approximately 200,000 people were killed. In addition to the murders and deaths, bandits and anyone with more guns or power stole land from their rightful owners, leading to a "large scale of socioeconomic dislocation" (Bell-Villada 27). Eventually, both sides admitted there had been too much disorder and loss of lives and order, and most people at first welcomed the June 13, 1953 *coup d'etat* by General Gustavo Rojas Pinilla, who touted a populist program.

For García Márquez, the night of rioting awoke him to the political turmoil in his country, and at the same time, affected the direction of his fiction. "That afternoon and evening, I became aware of the kind of country I was living in, and how little my short stories had to do with any of that. When I was later forced to go back to Barranquilla on the Caribbean, where I had spent my childhood, I realized that that was the type of life I had lived, knew, and wanted to write about" (Stone 321).

The ongoing political clashes and violence of his country certainly affected his fictional subjects, and works such as *No One Writes to the Colonel* (1961) and *In Evil Hour* (1962) were directly influenced by *la violencia*. He developed as a writer during one of the most violent periods in modern Colombia; however, he also spent the most violent of the years away from the nation's capital. At this point, the coastal region, where he lived, remained relatively peaceful. The move back to the coast played a part in shaping his fiction, and allowed him to reconnect to his Caribbean roots.

At the Universidad de Cartagena, García Márquez resumed his law studies. He performed with mediocrity, until he gradually stopped attending school altogether and quit before finishing his degree. He spent most of his time reading and writing for a newspaper. The short story he had published in *El Espectador* had earned him enough literary recognition that he was offered a position at *El Universal*, a Cartagena newspaper. His first article appeared in May 1948. The twenty-year old García Márquez wrote a five hundred-word daily column, covering a range of topics from twins to astrology. As Minta notes, "This was the beginning of a long journalistic career which García Márquez continues to pursue to the present day, a career which has provided both material support and a forum for the expression and discussion of his political views" (40).

During these formative years, García Márquez read widely, wrote for the newspaper, and became part of the "Barranquilla Group," a group of intellectuals, artists, and writers who met up in the evenings to debate and discuss literature in the nearby town of Barranquilla. The informal group was run by Ramón Vinyes, an older, erudite Catalonian book dealer who had written many unpublished plays and stories in

Catalan. Other members included Alfonso Fuenmayor, Germán Vargas, and Álvaro Samudio Cepeda, the latter who would become a novelist. This period was crucial in providing an opportunity for García Márquez to form his identity as a writer: "The contact with other people who were interested in writing, the possibility of regular discussion, the opportunity to discover new areas of literature, all were significant of his future development" (Minta 45). Vinyes, the informal leader of the group, introduced his followers to modernism, and incited in them an admiration for the work of William Faulkner, Virginia Woolf, and Ernest Hemingway. García Márquez was inspired by Woolf's use of interior monologue, which he believed was superior to that of Joyce. Furthermore, though García Márquez praised Kafka's for inciting him to write, he has credited William Faulkner's fiction with enabling him to discover that he wanted to become a writer. García Márquez felt that Faulkner's famous Yoknapatawpha County resembled Colombia. He told Rita Guibert in a 1971 interview that Faulkner's setting was "very much like my world, that it was created by the same people ... One mustn't forget that Faulkner is in a way a Latin American writer. His world is that of the Gulf of Mexico. What I found in him was affinities between our experiences, which were not as different as might appear at first sight" (327). García Márquez studied Faulkner's narrative techniques, themes, and small town settings. During these apprentice years, García Márquez read as much literature as he could. For example, when he fell sick with pneumonia, he was bedridden in his parents' house and he used the time to read. He devoured the Modernists and the works of the ancient Greeks, such as *Antigone* and *Oedipus Rex*, the latter which he has also cited as an important book in his life: "I've been astonished by its absolute perfection" (Guibert 317).

García Márquez began taking himself seriously as a writer, and after three years of studying law, abandoned his studies and rejected a possible career in law. At the start of 1950, he moved to Barranquilla and worked as a staff writer for the large coastal newspaper *El Heraldo*. He again wrote a column, this one called "La jirafa" ("The Giraffe"), and signed his work "Septimus," after the shell-shocked character in Virginia Woolf's *Mrs. Dalloway*. His columns expressed light humor, quirky observations, and irony.

In addition to the country's volatile political climate and his career change, there was something else that significantly affected García

Márquez during this period. In 1950, his grandmother died. At age twenty-two, García Márquez returned to Aracataca with his mother to take care of selling the family home. He was dismayed to learn that in her old age, his beloved grandmother had grown demented and blind, and the house had become decayed and dilapidated. The return trip to his magical childhood home left a lasting impression on García Márquez, calling up old memories and later inspiring him to start a long narrative titled "La casa" ("The House"). Although he would abandon the story, the idea would stay with him, brewing in his imagination for many years until he transformed the recollections into fiction. In García Márquez's view, returning to the house was "an event that influenced my literary tendencies." He further explained, "What really happened to me in that trip to Aracataca was that I realized that everything that had occurred in my childhood had a literary value that I was only now appreciating. From the moment I wrote *Leaf Storm* I realized I wanted to be a writer and that nobody could stop me and that the only thing left for me to try to be was the best writer in the world" (Stone 321). The visit to Aracataca impacted García Márquez on several levels. Most poignantly, perhaps, was that the town did not appear as magical and mythical as he had remembered it—instead Aracataca seemed dusty, hot, and desolate. His grandparents' house also had lost its magic. The critic Michael Bell focuses on Aracataca's symbolism of childhood, and how this return trip played an important role in nudging García Márquez to write about the past: "The memory of his lost childhood, itself mixed up with a sense of region and history, was of crucial importance to him" (6). After this trip, he would never again return to his childhood home.

Upon his return to Barranquilla, García Márquez began working seriously on his first novel. During the afternoons he would write the column for *El Heraldo*, and after closing time, he worked on a novel that would eventually become *La hojarasca* (*Leaf Storm*). When he finished writing for the evening, he would join his friends at the bars for discussions about literature. In *Leaf Storm*, he had begun to create the world of Macondo. At one point, he sent the novel to the prestigious Argentine publisher, Losada. The book's rejection letter included a note by Guillermo de Torre, the brother-in-law of the writer Jorge Luis Borges, in which de Torre "noted García Márquez's meager talents and suggested he try some other line of work" (Bell-Villada 142).

In 1950 and 1951, García Márquez became involved in launching and running two new magazines, *Crónica*, a weekly that survived for a year, and *Comprimido*, which survived only two issues. In his early twenties, García Márquez was securing his future career as a journalist. His interest in magazines and newspapers would remain with him throughout his life, and his role in the start up of these two magazines symbolized, according to Minta, the beginning of "a life-long commitment to the development of new outlets for creative journalism in Colombia, to counteract what he had always felt to be the crippling uniformity of the established Colombia press" (47).

Journalism helped García Márquez to better understand the techniques of narrative, the importance of specific details, and the structure of a story. García Márquez felt that both his journalism and fiction were equally crucial to his development as a writer: "I think the influence is reciprocal. Fiction has helped my journalism because it has given it literary value. Journalism has helped my fiction because it has kept me in a close relationship with reality" (Stone 322).

Though he was paid for his daily column, García Márquez was still quite poor. He lived in a brothel, sleeping in whatever vacant room he could find when he came in after his literary drinking sessions. On the days that he was short on money to pay for his room, he would leave his manuscript, *Leaf Storm*, as security. The prostitutes treated him as family and occasionally had lunch with him. During these bohemian years, he lived a carefree lifestyle, thriving on the social and cultural activity around him. He wrote columns during the day, worked on his novel in the evenings, and drank and socialized late into the night. Thin and wiry, the young García Márquez smoked constantly—forty cigarettes a day. He also read and wrote voraciously, and established long-lasting friendships.

García Márquez stayed with *El Heraldo* for three years. In 1953, he left his position at the newspaper and went through a period of transition. He held a variety of jobs, including a stint selling encyclopedias. Though he was not writing much during this time, he continued to educate himself by reading widely and deeply. As he developed his literary tastes, he began to figure out what he wanted to write about.

Traveling to Europe

In February 1954, at age twenty-six, García Márquez returned to Bogotá to work as a staff writer for *El Espectador*, the same newspaper where he had published his first short story. He covered a variety of stories and also served as the first regular film critic in Colombia. As time passed, he became more involved in investigative reporting. His editor, Jóseé Salgar, remembered García Márquez as being "a bit uncouth ... and very shy," and claimed that he "would arrive with bags under his eyes and his hair uncombed" (Paternostro, section III).

García Márquez's journalism career was beginning to thrive, and in 1955, his first novel, *Leaf Storm*, was published, marking the beginning of his literary career. Unfortunately, it was not as an impressive beginning as he had hoped. The novel was published by a small press, and when the owner disappeared, García Márquez took on the responsibility of selling the copies himself and paying off the printers. More proof of his literary talents arrived when he was awarded by the Association of Artists and Writers of Bogotá for one of his short stories.

Although his position at *El Espectador* provided García Márquez with more prestige and income than he had earned at *El Heraldo*, in general, his articles were not as lively or as quirky as they had been at the smaller newspaper. However, one particular story, published in a series of fourteen articles, brought him recognition and possibly played a hand in the closing of the liberal newspaper. The series focused on a twenty-year-old sailor, Luis Alejandro Velasco, the only survivor on a Navy destroyer after all of his companions were washed overboard. García Márquez spent many hours interviewing Velasco, and he wrote the story in first person, signing Velasco's name and not his own. García Márquez captured the tale in a series of fourteen installments, fascinating readers and increasing the newspaper's circulation. His use of suspense and specific details exposed his literary talents. When one of the articles revealed that the destroyer had been carrying contraband, the story sparked controversy. The dictatorship of Rojas Pinilla had already been threatening the newspaper's survival, and this article further provoked the government.

In 1955, trying to steer him away from trouble, *El Espectador* sent García Márquez on location to Geneva. The newspaper assigned him to cover the four-power summit conference, and also to be on location to cover the story of Pope Pius XII's imminent death (the latter did not happen, as the Pope lived for three more years). When he left Colombia, García Márquez's career in journalism was thriving, and according to Bell-Villada, "By mid-1955 García Márquez was arguably the most

renowned newspaper man in Colombia, and his time served overseas—
it has been said—would mercifully rescue him from the trap of local
journalistic fame" (51).

García Márquez did not return to Colombia right away. He
worked as a correspondent for the newspaper, earning a steady income
that allowed him to explore Europe. He traveled to Poland and
Hungary, and he enrolled for a short time at the Centro Sperimentale di
Cinema in Rome, where he studied film. García Márquez has always
expressed an interest in the medium of film and later would try his hand
at screenplay writing.

Everything seemed to be going well for his career as a journalist,
until he moved to Paris in January 1956 and discovered that the
Colombian dictator, Rojas Pinilla, had finally shut down *El Espectador*.
Although at first many had been pleased with Pinilla's government's
suppression of violence, eventually violence and repression returned
under his rule—including the crack-down on Liberal guerillas, the
massacre of protesting students, and the censorship of news. Pinilla
would finally be pressured by the military to resign in 1957.

El Espectador offered to buy García Márquez a return ticket home,
but instead, he pocketed the money and stayed in Paris to write full time.
He lived in the Latin Quarter and worked on what would turn into two
separate books—*In Evil Hour* and *No One Writes to the Colonel* (which he
rewrote eleven times). Both of these books emerged from the volatile
political situation he had witnessed in Colombia and were more
outwardly political than his first novel. "This was the time when the
relationship between literature and politics was very much discussed,"
he explained. "I kept trying to close the gap between the two" (Stone
323). He has called the books "journalistic literature," in which his style
of writing was now more influenced by Hemingway than by Faulkner.

While living in Paris, García Márquez experienced an
unforgettable moment when, one rainy day, he saw one of his literary
heroes, Ernest Hemingway, walking on the Boulevard St. Michel.
García Márquez was not sure whether he should approach him to
express his admiration or ask for an interview. But not wanting the
moment to be "spoiled," he did neither. Instead, he yelled from across
the street, "Maaaeeestro!" According to García Márquez, "Ernest
Hemingway understood that there could be no other master amid the
multitude of students, and he turned, raised his hand and shouted to me

in Castillian in a very childish voice, "Adiooos, amigo!" It was the only time I saw him" (*The New York Times* 1).

Living in poverty, García Márquez stayed in a small hotel where he survived on credit. He was gaunt and thin, and when his mother saw a photograph of him that he sent home, she lamented, "Poor Gabito. He looks like a skeleton" (Bell-Villada 52). He did not hold a regular job, and to make money, he scoured for bottles to turn in for deposits. Eventually, he managed to land a few freelance projects for a weekly published in Caracas, Venezuela, that his friend Plinio Apuleyo Mendoza edited. García Márquez had first met Mendoza, a fellow Colombian journalist, during his student days in Bogotá.

In addition to the occasional freelance projects, he spent most of his time working on his manuscript. This period in Europe marked the first time during which he worked almost exclusively, and extensively, on his fiction. Though hard at work, García Márquez did not isolate himself from reality. He lived in Paris during the French war in Algeria, and it has been widely rumored, although the details are obscure, that he worked for the Algerian National Liberation Front and also spent a short time in jail (Bell-Villada 52).

Although the period in France was invaluable to his development as a writer, García Márquez was not impressed by the country—at least not in terms of its politics and social structure. Feeling very much like an outsider, he observed the workings of the country from a distant perspective. Stephen Minta attests that García Márquez's general impression of western Europe was that it "seemed to be in a state of terminal decline" (50), and he remained uninterested in its culture. On the other hand, he was attracted to the workings of the socialist countries to the east. While he was in Europe, he visited several of these countries, carefully studying their culture, governments, and societies. In March of 1957, he traveled with his friend Mendoza to observe the Soviet Union, East Germany, and Czechoslovakia.

Traveling to these countries provided him with an intimate view of the workings of socialism and communism. While he expressed admiration for Soviet achievements, he finally rejected the Soviet model after his extensive travels. García Márquez has favored and been closely tied to the Communist party, yet he admits in the same breath that he was disillusioned by the communism of the Soviet Union. The trips to these countries brought García Márquez more insight and strengthened his support for socialism. As Stephen Minta explains, when García Márquez traveled to these socialist countries, he "believed then, as he has always done, that socialism is the only system capable of resolving the vastly unequal distribution of wealth that is one of the basic causes of poverty throughout Latin America, and so he went to the socialist countries of eastern Europe with a willingness to learn" (52). Though García Márquez has always supported socialism, he also espouses complex political views and has been the target of much controversy. However, he remains true to his individualistic political beliefs: "Criticized by orthodox Communists and neoconservatives both, he remains above the fray, refusing to get involved in vicious polemics or to respond to dishonest attacks" (Bell-Villada 66). The most apt way to describe García Márquez's politics is to consider him an independent Leftist, as well as a dedicated socialist. In 1971, he told Guibert, "I think the world ought to be socialist, that it will be, and that we should help this to happen as quickly as possible" (329).

In the fall of 1957, after these extensive travels, García Márquez moved to London where he hoped to study English. However, he found London to be cold and gray, and he missed his tropical homeland. In spite of his international traveling and political controversies, García Márquez has always called Latin America his home and feels quite connected to his cultural roots. "In general terms, I feel that I'm a native of any country in Latin America but not anywhere else," he explained (Stone 334). When Mendoza offered him a position at the new weekly newspaper, *Momento*, in Venezuela, García Márquez decided it was time to leave Europe and to go home to Latin America.

REVOLUTION

García Márquez left Europe in December 1957 and flew to Caracas, Venezuela, arriving to the country during a time of radical transition. The dictatorship of General Marcos Pérez Jiménez, which had begun in 1948, was in its final collapsing weeks. Everyday, uprisings and explosive speeches threatened the dictator's power. Trying to hold on to its last days, the dictatorship set curfews and conducted police raids. When the offices of *Momento* were raided, the police arrested everyone there; García Márquez escaped only because he happened to be out of the office at the time.

The dictatorship ended and a few months later, in March, García Márquez made a trip back to Colombia. He went to Barranquilla and married Mercedes Barcha Pardo, the daughter of a pharmacist, who he had met years ago. Mercedes, of Egyptian origin, had turned into a tall, striking woman. García Márquez had first met her when she was thirteen-years-old, in Sucre, when he was a college student visiting his parents for the holidays. He told the story of their early "engagement" to his friend Plinio Apuleyo Mendoza:

> One day, at a student dance, I asked her to marry me. Looking back I think the proposal was a metaphorical way of getting round all the fuss and bother you had to go through in those days to get a girlfriend. She must have understood it this way because we saw each other very sporadically, always very casually, but I think neither of us had any doubt that sooner or later the metaphor would become fact. It actually became fact some ten years after the fiction, without ever really having been engaged. We were just two people waiting, unhurriedly and imperturbably, for the inevitable. (22)

After they married, they returned to Venezuela. While there, García Márquez wrote most of the stories that would make up *Los funerales de la Mamá Grande* (*Big Mama's Funeral*). He eventually resigned from *Momento* over a dispute about the magazine's support for U.S. Vice-President Nixon. During Nixon's visit to Venezuela, there had been popular demonstrations against him. In response, the editor of *Momento* had printed an apologetic editorial to Nixon and the U.S., an apology which García Márquez opposed.

For a short time, he wrote for another Venezuelan paper, but soon a better opportunity emerged. At the time, the Latin American world was in a state of major change. After the right-winged dictatorships had fallen in both Venezuela and Colombia, the defeat of Cuba's dictator Fulgencio Batista followed. Fidel Castro had secretly returned to Cuba from exile, and with a small group of followers, including Che Guevara, he fought against the corrupt, brutal regime of Batista. On January 8, 1959, Castro and his supporters entered Havana in triumph.

García Márquez was one of the journalists invited to Fidel Castro's

"Operation Truth," a media campaign that countered the U.S. media's coverage of these events. When the Cuban government launched the news agency, Prensa Latina, García Márquez, moved to Bogotá with Mercedes, who was pregnant at the time, to work for the news agency's Colombian branch. The agency wanted to create an alternative source of news about Cuba, to counteract what was being reported in the international community.

Like many Latin American intellectuals and writers, García Márquez favored the socialist Revolution. During this exciting period of political and cultural changes, a great amount of Latin American literature appeared, helping to create the "boom." Although the success of the Latin novel had already been recognized in Latin America, it was not until the 1960s that it was recognized with such fervor in the international world. García Márquez noted, "The great cultural importance of Cuba in Latin America has been to serve as a kind of bridge to transmit a type of literature which had existed in Latin America for many years. In a sense, the boom in Latin American literature in the United States has been caused by the Cuban Revolution ... When the Cuban Revolution started there was suddenly a great interest about Cuba and Latin America" (Stone 335).

Unlike many artists and writers who later changed their views about the Castro regime, García Márquez has always supported the Revolution: "García Márquez's enthusiasm for the Cuban Revolution has remained undiminished to the present day, and, if he has had some private reservations about the direction which the revolution has taken, he has never doubted that its achievements have been of far greater significance than its limitations" (Minta 59). Cuba rose up as an inspiration against colonialism, exploitation, and the economic dependence of the region upon the United States.

García Márquez had been committed several years of vigorous journalist activity in support of the Revolution. In addition to his position at Prensa Latina, he also helped launch *Acción Liberal*, a magazine published in Bogotá, in hope of stirring up the Colombian left.

The same year as the Revolution, Mercedes gave birth to a son, Rodrigo. García Márquez identified as an atheist; however, at that time, in order for a child to be officially recognized in Colombia, he had to be baptized. García Márquez called on one of his oldest friends from the National University, Camilo Torres, to perform the baptism. A militant priest, Torres agreed to baptize the baby, though he expressed anger that nobody kneeled during the ceremony. García Márquez felt little respect for priests, but he held deep admiration for Torres—he was an activist, committed to socialism, and later became one of the most popular political leaders in Colombia. Eventually, in 1965, Torres would leave the priesthood to join the leftist guerrilla organization, the Army of National Liberation. Comprised of mostly student radicals, this group imitated Castro's guerrilla fighters and focused its activities in the countryside. A year after joining, Torres died in combat against the Colombian army.

After the birth of his son, García Márquez moved with his family to Havana, Cuba, for six months to continue working for Prensa Latina. In 1960, they relocated to New York City to work in the agency's U.S. branch office. The socialist government of Cuba was beginning to come under attack by Cuban exiles and the United States, and in January, 1961, diplomatic relations between Cuba and the U.S. broke off completely. As a supporter of the Revolution, García Márquez was often threatened by right-wing Cuban exiles in New York. Once, while driving home to his apartment in Queens, a car pulled up beside him and a passenger pointed a gun at him. For safety, he kept an iron rod by his desk.

Though he only lived in New York for six months, García Márquez was impressed with the city's energy and diversity. He once described New York as "the greatest phenomenon of the twentieth century." He explained, "The United States is an extraordinary country; a nation that creates such a city as New York, or the rest of the country— which has nothing to do with the system or the government—could do anything. I believe they will be the ones to create a great socialist revolution, and a good one too" (Guibert 335). Yet he also knew he could not permanently live there: "I doubt if I have strong enough nerve to live in New York. I find it so overwhelming" (Guibert 335).

He resigned from Prensa Latina in 1961 when a friend was fired from the agency. After the Bay of Pigs invasion, the Cuban government had entered a contentious period, and tensions were rising within the revolutionary party itself. After resigning from Prensa Latina, García Márquez and his family took a long Greyhound bus trip to the south in an "homage to Faulkner." He had always wanted to see the hot, dusty, and poverty-stricken place that his literary hero had immortalized, and the trip provided evidence "of the similarity between our two worlds" (Guibert 327). However, García Márquez's family also experienced the racism of the South. Perceived as Mexicans, they were repeatedly denied lodging.

García Márquez had only $100 in his pocket and a $120 uncashed check, but he managed to get across the border to Mexico City. He hoped to write film scripts there, but was unable to find immediate work. Instead, he took a job as an editor-in-chief for two popular glossy magazines, *Sucesos* and *La Familia*.

In 1961, at age thirty-three, García Márquez won the Esso Prize, a literary prize in Mexico, for *La mala hora* (*In Evil Hour*), after his friends convinced him to submit the novel. Both *In Evil Hour* and *No One Writes to the Colonel* (which he had finished writing while in France) were novels inspired by *la violencia* and dealt directly with the politics of Latin America. After winning the contest, *In Evil Hour* was published in Spain; however, the publishing house changed all of the slang and informal words to "correct Castilian," irrevocably transforming the entire style and voice of the novel. García Márquez rejected the edition, and when the book was republished many years later in the original text, he provided a note of explanation about the different versions.

That same year, in 1962, his second son, Gonzalo, was born, and *No One Writes to the Colonel* and the collected stories of *Big Mama's Funeral* were published—the latter almost by accident. García Márquez had actually completed the stories a few years prior, but had made little effort to submit the stories to publishers. They were absently passed around amongst his friends, until one of those friends, Álvaro Celestino Mutis, who had read them while in prison in Mexico City, found a publisher for the collection. García Márquez received one thousand pesos (about one hundred U.S. dollars at the time), and 2,000 copies were printed. He dedicated the book to Mercedes.

He worked for the glossy magazines *Sucesos* and *La Familia* until 1963, when he quit to begin working for the Mexican branch of the J. Walter Thompson advertising agency. While working full-time, he also managed to break into the world of cinema. He wrote approximately two dozen film scripts in two years, most of them melodramas filled with shoot-outs and duels, and some of them in collaboration with the Mexican novelist Carlos Fuentes. He later said in an interview that he much preferred the independence of creating fiction versus the collaboration that comes with writing film scripts: "So many interests, so many compromises are involved that in the end very little of the original story remains. Whereas if I shut myself in my room I can write exactly what I want to. I don't have to put up with an editor saying, 'Get rid of that character or incident and put in another'" (Guibert 321).

From 1962–1965, García Márquez was not writing any fiction. According to the Peruvian novelist Mario Vargas Llosa, the publication of *In Evil Hour* had greatly displeased him and "his disappointment resulted in a literary silence which lasted for a few years. He thought that perhaps he would never be able to write the novel of which he dreamed; he decided, in all probability, to forget about Macondo" (16). Approaching forty, García Márquez suffered a severe bout of writer's block, and adamantly told a friend, "I'll never write again" (Bell-Villada 56). The Chilean novelist José Donoso recalls seeking out García Márquez at a party, eager to meet the man who was beginning to be known in small literary circles, and being told that he "was experiencing a literary dry spell, one that had lasted for nearly ten years" (96–97). Donosco described the virtually unknown writer as "a gloomy, melancholy person tormented by his writer's block" (97).

The Magic of Inspiration

One afternoon in 1965, García Márquez was driving along the Mexico-City-Acapulco highway, and according to him, he realized quite suddenly that he could envision his next novel—he could plainly see every single word of the book he had been wanting to write for years. "It was so ripe in me that I could have dictated the first chapter, word by word, to a typist" (Bell-Villada 56).

He made a fast U-turn and returned to his house. He asked Mercedes to handle the family finances and household needs for the next six months, and then he went into seclusion to write. He wrote for eight hours everyday in his room, which his family called "the Cave of the Mafia," armed with an endless supply of coffee and cigarettes on hand. Mercedes had built the room for him, which was so small that only his table and chair could fit.

García Márquez had finally broken through the writer's block and seized upon this inspiration. "There comes a moment when all obstacles fade away, all conflict disappears, things you never dreamt of occur to you and, at that moment, there is absolutely nothing in the world better than writing," he admitted to his colleague Mendoza. "That is what I would call inspiration" (*Guava* 34). Though he worked in solitude, he still liked to consult his closest friends on the manuscript. He showed the first three chapters to Carlos Fuentes, who wrote a praising, laudatory reaction in a Mexican magazine.

As García Márquez devoted all of his time and energy to writing the novel, the family grew so desperate for money that Mercedes started pawning their belongings, including the TV, a radio, and an eggbeater. She also borrowed money from friends and arranged for loans. García Márquez's requested six months had turned into eighteen months. When he finally finished the manuscript and emerged from his "cave," the family was $10,000 in debt. Yet he had in hand 1,300 typed pages of a completed manuscript. About 5,000 pages of drafts and revisions had been tossed in the garbage.

After six years of literary silence, García Márquez had written his fourth novel, *Cien años de soledad* (*One Hundred Years of Solitude*). Earlier in the year, a publisher in Argentina had agreed look at his novel-in-progress, so now García Márquez and Mercedes prepared the manuscript to be mailed. When they were walking to the post office, the manuscript box fell open and pages began to fly around the street. Once they gathered the pages, they realized that they did not have enough money to pay the full postage. García Márquez mailed out only half of the novel, then returned home to come up with the rest of the money. He sent the rest of the novel out that afternoon. Later Mercedes admitted that she was worried that after all the financial and emotional hardships, nothing would happen: "And what if, after all this, it's a bad novel?" (Bell-Villada 57).

However, the publishers accepted the novel, and when they sent him the galley proofs to be proofread, García Márquez changed only one word, though he was encouraged to make as many changes as he wished. This epic story had been spinning itself in his mind for so long that when he finally constructed it into a novel, he felt confident that, by this point, no mistakes had been made. Though he threw away many pages during the process of writing the novel, he also constructed his lines carefully. About his work habits, he explained, "And now I've acquired a habit which I think is a vice. I correct line by line as a I work, so that by the time a page is finished it's practically ready for the publisher. If it has a blot or a slip it won't do for me" (Guibert 324).

García Márquez had immersed himself so fully in the writing of this book that when he finished, he was emotionally and intellectually drained. Much of the myths, histories, and legends of Macondo had emerged from the stories he remembered being told when he was growing up in Aracataca. His friend Eduardo Márceles Daconte attests, "Gabo remembers those stories they used to tell—things that many people have forgotten. He has an elephant's memory" (Paternostro, section I). García Márquez became so involved in the lives of the characters, that he had actually cried when the character of Colonel Aureliano Buendía had to be killed off: "When I finished the chapter, I went up to Mercedes on the second floor of our house, trembling.... I lay down on my bed and cried for hours" (*Guava* 33).

García Márquez had researched numerous aspects of the novel, often consulting the *Encyclopedia Britannica*, as well as books on home medicines, disease, poison, alchemy, and navigation. After he sent off the manuscript, García Márquez cleaned out his desk of the numerous pages of notes, diagrams, and sketches that had helped him to create his masterpiece. He later explained he threw everything out "not only so that the way the book was constructed shouldn't be known—that's something absolutely private—but in case that material should ever be sold. To sell it would be selling my soul, and I'm not going to let anyone do it, not even my children" (Guibert 326).

García Márquez expected modest sales and perhaps good reviews, but he never dreamed of what was in store for him. *One Hundred Years of Solitude* first appeared in Buenos Aires, Argentina, in 1967, and in Vargas Llosa's words, its arrival provoked "a literary earthquake throughout Latin America" (5). The publisher began with a printing of 8,000 copies, far more than any of García Márquez's others novels, and then quickly added new editions. The novel was so popular with both critics and the public that at one point, new editions were appearing once a week. In Latin America, García Márquez had become famous "overnight," and was "almost as famous as a great soccer player or an eminent singer of boleros" (Vargas Llosa 5).

For the first time in his life, García Márquez's fiction earned him financial independence. He liked to remark that he was forty-years old and had already published four other books before he ever collected any royalties on his work. Over the next two years, his fame would grow exponentially, not only in Latin America but throughout the international community. Sales of *One Hundred Years* skyrocketed, and awards and honors rained over him. Today, he is the most widely-read novelist in Spanish, and one of the most acclaimed modern novelists in the world.

One Hundred Years of Solitude chronicles the saga of the Buendías living in the mythical town of Macondo, based on the place where García Márquez grew up—Aracataca. The novel had been swelling inside of him since he was in his early twenties, when he attempted to write a story entitled "La casa," but at that point in his life, he had "neither the vital experience nor the literary means" to complete such a rich, profound work (Guibert 306). Macondo also appeared in several stories in *Big Mama's Funeral*, though it was sometimes called by a different name. Recurrences of characters and events, and cross-referencing of Macondo occurs throughout García Márquez's fiction, yet it was *One Hundred Years of Solitude* that brought Macondo into full realization, and made it a household name in many Latin American homes.

Before García Márquez ever sat down to write the story of Macondo, the myths and legends of the town had entered his consciousness and stimulated his imagination as a small child. García Márquez explained how his fiction changed direction after the first publication of *The Evil Hour*, which at first seemed more political than *One Hundred Years of Solitude*: "[W]hen I finished *The Evil Hour*, I saw that all my views were wrong again. I came to see that in fact my writings about my childhood were *more* political and had more to do with the reality of my country than I had thought" (Stone 323). García Márquez had known for a long time that he wanted to write about Aracataca, but he had struggled with the novel's tone and structure:

> I had an idea of what I always wanted to do, but there was something missing and I was not sure what it was until one day I discover the right tone—the tone that I eventually used in *One Hundred Years of Solitude*. It was based on the way my grandmother used to tell her stories. She told things that sounded supernatural and fantastic, but she told them with complete naturalness. When I finally discovered the tone I had to use, I sat down for eighteen months and worked everyday. (Stone 323)

Critics have praised the novel for its depth and imaginative writing. Vargas Llosa admires the book's artistic and popular achievement and "its capacity for being at one time things which were thought to be opposites: traditional and modern, regional and universal; imaginary and realistic. Yet perhaps the most mysterious of the virtues is the third: its unlimited accessibility; that is its power to be within anyone's reach, with distinct but abundant rewards for everyone" (5). *One Hundred Years of Solitude* not only excited critics, but quickly won over the mainstream reading public. In Colombia, people from all socio-economic classes were reading the book; the book was not, unlike many other literary novels, directed toward a literary elite. Eventually, the novel was translated into over thirty languages and became an international hit. In Soviet Russia, the book quickly sold a million copies (the sex scenes, however, were censored). One elderly Soviet woman felt so amazed and moved by the book that when she finished reading it, she then "copied out the entire text of the novel word by word, in order to make sure that she had really read what she had read" (Bell-Villada 4). The novel captured success in every way, delighting critics, fellow authors, and the mainstream public.

With this novel, critics also began to speak about "magic realism," a movement that is often credited to García Márquez, although the technique appeared earlier, most notably in the work of Alejo Carpentier. When he was working on the novel, García Márquez did not set out to write a "magic realist" novel. He simply wanted to capture the stories of his grandmother without leaving the realm of reality. He has often said that if a writer makes something specific enough, he can make the reader believe anything, no matter how fantastic or exaggerated. For example, he told Peter Stone that he struggled with the scene of Remedios the Beauty ascending to heaven. Then one day he went outside and saw a woman hanging up the sheets to dry on a windy day: "I discovered that if I used the sheets for Remedios the Beauty, she would ascend. That's how I did it, to make it credible. The problem for every writer is credibility. Anybody can write anything so long as it's believed" (324).

Voice and tone have also helped García Márquez create this sense of credibility. When he wrote the novel, he thought about the way his grandmother told her stories about the supernatural. "What was the most important was the expression she had on her face. She did not change her expression at all when telling her stories, and everyone was surprised," he explained. "In previous attempts to write *One Hundred Years of Solitude*, I tried to tell the story without believing in it. I discovered that what I had to do was believe in them myself and write them with the same expression with which my grandmother told them: with a brick face" (Stone 324).

Despite the "magical" aspect of his work, García Márquez dismisses fantasy as something simplistic and cliché. He argues that his work is always ground in reality, and that imagination differs from fantasy. "Everyday life in Latin American proves that reality is full of the most extraordinary things," he explains (*Guava* 35). In addition to his grandmother's method of telling stories, journalism also influenced his writing style: "Journalism taught me ways of lending my stories authenticity" (*Guava* 32). Reporting also wed him to reality: "That's why I have always tried to keep on doing journalism, because it keeps me in contact with the real world, particularly political journalism and politics" (Stone 328).

García Márquez was not the only writer to be experimenting with forms of realism and narrative structure. In the 1940s and 50s, prominent Latin American authors reacted against traditional narrative form, including Aldofo Bioy Casares, Jorge Luis Borges, Alejo Carpentier, inspiring the next generation of writers, such as García Márquez, Carlos Fuentes, Mario Vargas Llosa, and Julio Cortázar. Latin American literature exploded in the '60s, and though many authors were important during this period, it was *One Hundred Years of Solitude* that truly captured international attention. Another novelist of the "Boom" period, José Donoso, admits that only with *One Hundred Years of Solitude* "can one talk about a 'triumph' in a popular and commercial sense" (56). He explains, "Before *One Hundred* and despite the proportionally greater success of other writers of the Boom, the success had been, more than anything else, literary, confined to an elite, each time more extensive, certainly, but always an elite" (56). García Márquez's work rapidly moved beyond the literary circles, pleasing critics as well as popular readers. Critic Raymond L. Williams attests, "With [*One Hundred Year's of Solitude's*] publication, García Márquez both reaffirmed the author's right of invention and produced one of the finest examples of transcendent regionalism in the Spanish-American tradition" (156). Clearly, *One Hundred Years of Solitude's* critical acclaim and popularity would forever change García Márquez's life.

SEARCHING FOR SECLUSION

The extraordinary success of *One Hundred Years of Solitude* was exciting for García Márquez, but also overwhelming. Reporters pursued García Márquez for interviews and women sent photographs of themselves. He felt he could not continue to work in Mexico City because he was too famous, and the interviews, phone calls, and fan mail took up too much of his time. To escape the commotion, García Márquez and his family moved to Barcelona, Spain in October 1967.

Now in Barcelona, he felt ready to begin his next fiction project—a book about a dictator and his fall from power. The idea first came to him when he was living in Caracas and watched the fall of the dictator General Marcos Pérez Jiménez, and the idea continued to grow when García Márquez was covering the Cuban Revolution and witnessed the trial of Batista's notorious Army major Jesús Sosa Blanco. He had been shocked as he listened to the criminal's long list of crimes. García Márquez had tried to write this book earlier, then abandoned it: "I stopped writing *The Autumn of the Patriarch* in Mexico in 1962 when I'd done about 300 pages, and the only thing that survived was the name of the main character" (Guava 34).

As with *One Hundred Years of Solitude*, the story of *The Autumn of the Patriarch* needed time to brew. He read, observed, and researched before writing the novel: "I read everything that I could find about Latin America dictators of the last century, and the beginning of this one. I also talked to a lot of people who had lived under dictatorships. I did that for at least ten years," he explained. "And when I had a clear idea of what the character was going to be like, I made an effort to forget everything I had read or heard, so that I could invent, without using any situation that had occurred in real life" (Stone 327).

Though García Márquez's Latin American background had provided him with exposure to many dictators, he realized he had not lived for a long period of time under a dictatorship. So he moved to Spain not only to get away from all of the publicity in Mexico, but also to conduct research—he wanted to observe the right-wing dictatorship of General Francisco Franco up close.

While he was living in Spain, García Márquez become friends with the Peruvian novelist Mario Vargas Llosa. At this time, Spain was home to several expatriate Latin American writers. Vargas Llosa would later write the first biography of the novelist, *García Márquez: Historia de un deicidio* (1971), a 650-page study of García Márquez and *One Hundred Years of Solitude*.

While the move to Spain allowed García Márquez to directly observe a right-wing dictatorship, the country's political atmosphere and geographical climate was not quite right for his book, which takes place in Latin America. He explained that although the move to Europe was helpful, he needed the setting of the Caribbean:

> I found that the atmosphere was very different in Spain under Franco from that of a Caribbean dictatorship. So the book was kind of blocked for about a year. There was something missing and I wasn't sure what it was. Then overnight, I decided that the best thing was to come back to the Caribbean.... As I went from island to island, I found the elements which were the ones that had been lacking from my novel. (Stone 327).

The regime of Franco seemed cold and repressive; García Márquez wanted to capture the flamboyance and excess that characterized many of the Latin American dictatorships. He also needed to reacquaint himself with a tropical setting. So he returned to Colombia for a year to observe the country, then went back to Spain to finish writing the novel: "When I got back to Barcelona where I was writing the book, I grew a few plants, added a few smells, and finally managed to convey the heat of a tropical city to the reader" (*Guava* 35).

Initially, García Márquez planned to write this novel in a year; it actually took seven. While working on this new book, his fame continued to burgeon at a rapid speed. In 1969, *One Hundred Years of Solitude* won the Chianchiano Prize in Italy and was named the Best Foreign Book in France. A year later, the novel was published in English and chosen as one of twelve best books of the year by U.S. critics.

In 1971, García Márquez was awarded an honorary doctorate from Columbia University. However, because he had worked for the Cuban news agency Prensa Latina during the Cuban Revolution, García Márquez was blacklisted and only issued a provisional visa. The U.S. government refused to grant García Márquez an extended visa, and he could only visit the United States for a specific length of time because of his communist affiliations.

García Márquez was surprised by the prestigious honorary doctorate:

> What I find completely puzzling and disconcerting is not the honor nor the recognition—although such things can be true—but that a university like Columbia should decide to choose me out of twelve men from the whole world. The last thing I ever expected in this world was a doctorate of letters. My path has always been anti-academic. (Guibert 336)

Furthermore, he claimed that giving him the honor was like "if they gave the Nobel Prize to a bullfighter" (Guibert 336). He considered refusing the honorary doctorate for these reasons, but his friends and family convinced him to accept the honor. Refusing to wear a suit and tie, he attended the ceremony and admitted later that he felt grateful. Many Latin Americans were in the audience, and when they called out, "Up with Latin America," García Márquez "felt moved and was glad [he] had accepted" (Guibert 337). He later said he felt "delighted" to be recognized with such honor, "on behalf of my country and Latin America" (336).

WRITING HABITS

García Márquez considers himself "not so much to be a writer as a story-teller" (Guibert 318). He describes himself as thinking and speaking in anecdotes and explained to the interviewer, Rita Guibert, that often a story arises from a single image or idea. For example, while he was writing *Autumn of the Patriarch*, he kept a notebook to jot down ideas for future stories. One of these ideas grew out of a single night in Barcelona, when the lights in his home went out. The electrician told García Márquez, "Light is like water," and "In that fraction of a second, a complete story came to me," claimed García Márquez (Guibert 318). He envisioned a story in which two young brothers "break an electric light bulb and the light begins to flow out—just like water—filling the house three feet deep. They take the boat and begin rowing through the bedrooms and the kitchen" (Guibert 319). García Márquez did not immediately write the story, but composed a brief note that read, "Children drowning in light." This story, "Light is Like Water," was later collected in *Strange Pilgrims: Twelve Stories* (1993).

Furthermore, once the idea arrives, he may research and develop it, but he does not set out to write a particular story: "There's nothing deliberate or predictable in all this, nor do I know when it's going to happen to me. I'm at the mercy of my imagination and that's what says *yes* or *no*" (Guibert 319). Yet at the same time, García Márquez works with outlines, and often conducts research for his work. He stresses that the sources for his material always arrive from imagination and life. Although he pays attention to his dreams, as his grandmother did, he believes, "that life itself is the greatest source of inspiration and that dreams are only a very small part of that torrent that is life" (Stone 331).

When writing, García Márquez believes in the necessity of solitude: "In fact, I believe writers are always alone, like ship-wrecked sailors in the middle of the ocean. It's the loneliness profession in the world. No one can help you write what you are writing" (*Guava* 30). He is also adamant about staying healthy; he never drinks or takes drugs while working: "To be a good writer you have to be absolutely lucid at every moment of writing, and in good health" (Stone 329).

Through his work, García Márquez hopes to move and entertain the reader, and does not want the reader to be disinterested: "I'm always in terror lest at some page the reader may get bored and throw down the book. Therefore I try not to bore him, so that he shan't treat me as I treat others" (Guibert 328). When working on a novel, he tends to "live my characters before writing them. I spoke the lines of the people in *Cien Años* for years before writing the book. I got to know them that way." (Rodman 129). Although such immersion in his characters contributes to the slow pace of his writing, he remains patient and focused: "If I'm writing a novel I can't mix other things with it, I must work at that book only, even if it takes me more than ten years" (Guibert 320).

The Autumn of the Patriarch, for example, took much longer than anyone, including García Márquez, had anticipated. He had hoped to write the book in one year, but it took seven. One reason García Márquez had trouble completing the book was that the immense success and popularity of *One Hundred Years of Solitude* added more pressure. He seemed genuinely surprised by the public's response to *One Hundred Years*, and soon found that the fame and the expectations of his large readership threatened to hinder his writing. In the midst of writing *The Autumn of the Patriarch*, García Márquez said in an interview, "I know that a lot of people are waiting for it. Every letter I write weighs me down, you can't imagine how much!" (Guibert 310). Furthermore, he stopped reading critical responses to his work because he felt the analyses were affecting his ability to write: "my work stopped being intuitive" (Guibert 313). He lamented that he used to write only for his wife and his friends, but when he was working on *Autumn*, he felt that his audience had grown large and abstract: "The problem after writing *One Hundred Years of Solitude* was that now I no longer know whom of the millions of readers I am writing for; this upsets and inhibits me. It's alike a million eyes are looking at you and you don't really know what they think" (Stone 322). García Márquez claimed that it was easier to write during his bohemian journalism days because then he was more carefree, whereas now, "[w]hat happens is simply that your sense of responsibility increases. You begin to feel that now each word you write carries more weight, that it influences many more people" (*Guava* 25).

Despite the pressure, García Márquez continued following his typical writing routine while working on *Autumn:* "I always wake very early, at about six in the morning. I read the paper in bed, get up, drink my coffee while I listen to music on the radio, and at about nine—after the boys have gone to school—I sit down to write" (Guibert 311). His work habits had also changed since his younger writing days. Whereas once he had written late at night above a dingy office, thriving on action and noise, now he craved quiet. He could no longer write in hotels or work on borrowed typewriters. Now his ideal writing place would be "a desert island in the mornings and a big city at night. In the morning I need silence, and in the evening a few drinks and some good friends to chat to" (*Guava* 30), and he prefers to work in "a quiet, well-heated room" (*Guava* 26).

As a very disciplined writer, routine is important for him. In the afternoon, he stops writing to take a long lunch around two o'clock with his family. A siesta usually follows. After he wakes from his nap, he likes to listen to music, preferring chamber music and popular Latin American songs. He told Rita Guibert that he enjoyed music "much more than any other manifestation of art, even than literature" (329). He attested, "My passion for music is like a secret vice, and I hardly ever talk about it. It's part of my most profoundly private life" (329).

Throughout his life, García Márquez has read voraciously, yet he does not revere books as precious objects. Until more recently, he never had a traditional library and expressed more interest for the story than the book itself. He claimed in a 1972 interview that after he read a book, he would leave it behind or toss it out. According to the interviewer Selden Rodman, once when Mercedes asked her husband to finish a book that she wanted to read, he simply tore the book in two and gave her the part he had already read (125). Furthermore, García Márquez does not limit himself to reading only literary fiction, and, in an interview in 1981, claimed to be reading very little fiction at all. At the time, he was mostly reading political books and publications about pop culture. He subscribed to *Time* magazine for at least twenty years, as well as many other magazines. He spoke at length about his interest in knowledge, including pop culture:

> I've lost this sacred notion of reading only 'literature.' I will read anything. I try to keep up to date. I read almost all the really important magazines from all over the world every week ... But after I've read all the serious and important newspapers from all over, my wife always comes around and tells me of news I hadn't heard. When I ask her where she read it, she will say she read it at a beauty parlor. So I read fashion magazines and all kinds of magazines for women and gossip magazines. And I learn many things I could only learn from reading them. That keeps me very busy." (Stone 336)

THE WORLD OF POLITICS

Eventually, García Márquez completed the novel that followed *One Hundred Years*. The long-awaited *The Autumn of The Patriarch* was published in 1975, ironically, the same year as General Franco's death. It quickly sold half a million copies; however, its dense, difficult prose turned off many readers, who were hoping to return to the magical world of Macondo. Structured in six unnumbered chapters, each comprised of a single sentence, it is a difficult book. García Márquez once described the novel "as a prose poem" (*Guava* 50). Unlike *One Hundred Years*, the book proved to be inaccessible to many readers, and critics also expressed disappointment. However, over time, opinion has

changed and many consider this novel to be a major work of García
Márquez's oeuvre, as well as Latin American fiction.

After the book was published, García Márquez bought a house in
Pedregal San Angel, a suburb of Mexico City in which luxury residencies
are built on volcanic rock, and he announced that *The Autumn of The
Patriarch* would be his last novel. He vowed that as long as the Augusto
Pinochet regime remained in power in Chile, he would publish no more
fiction and would devote himself entirely to journalism. Critic Stephen
Minta elaborates on this claim:

> The decision, of course, was an act of political protest, a
> reflection that, in circumstances as horrifying as those which
> followed the overthrow of democracy in Chile in 1973, a
> writer could not, in honesty, sit quietly at his desk creating
> fictions; but it also reflected a view, which García Márquez
> has held with varying degrees of intensity over the years, that
> journalism is a more powerful, because more immediate,
> weapon of education and persuasion than literature. (41)

Politics and social problems have always been important to García
Márquez, and as his fame grew, he learned he could use his journalism,
money, and his international reputation toward fighting for political
causes. For example, in 1972, García Márquez received the honorable
Rómulo Gallegos Prize in Venezuela, and at the ceremony, he publicly
donated the entire sum of $22,000 to the parliamentary Movimiento al
Socialismo (MAS), a Venezuelan socialist party. That same year, he also
gave his $10,000 Neustadt Prize to the Committee in Solidarity with
Political Prisoners. Bell-Villada points out that "García Márquez had
begun using his global fame as an instrument of support for left-wing
causes, or for 'quiet diplomacy' between warring parties" (58).

García Márquez's politics have often been difficult for the
international and Latin American public to pin down. Though his views
might be complex, García Márquez has always sided with the Left. He
has always been a dedicated supporter of Castro and the Cuban
Revolution, but has given different thoughts about his relationship to
Communism. For example, he told Mendoza, "I was more of a
sympathizer than a real militant. Since then my relationship with the
Communists has had many ups and downs. We've often been at

loggerheads because every time I adopt a stance they don't like, their newspapers really gave a go at me. But I've never publicly condemned them, even at the worst moments" (*Guava* 97). Yet when speaking to the U.S. press, he often distances himself from the communist party. Stephen Minta analyzes García Márquez's precarious position, explaining that North American circles have not been sympathetic toward his "socialist convictions," and that the U.S. press often tries to simplify and "to analyze all political activity in terms of right and left" (56). García Márquez's public statements are often contradictory or even misleading, further confusing people about his alliances, and also making it difficult for him to be pigeonholed. García Márquez defended his seemingly contradictory statements to Rita Guibert: "I've said that anyone who doesn't contradict himself is a dogmatist, and every dogmatist is a reactionary. I contradict myself all the time and particularly on the subject of literature" (322).

Minta observes that García Márquez's controversial position has "left himself open to the charge of being a political dilettante" (56). García Márquez has been criticized by Colombians, communists, the United States, and intellectuals. For example, because he has not openly aligned himself with the left-wing movements in Colombia (though he has expressed enthusiasm for other Latin American socialist parties), his devotion to local politics has often been scrutinized. He also has been the subject of controversy for his unflagging support for the Cuban Revolution. Many of the earlier supporters of the Cuban Revolution changed their affiliation with the arrest of the poet Herberto Padilla in 1971. Castro had jailed Padilla for "counterrevolutionary activity," and this move caused many supporters to break with the Revolution. Although García Márquez was dismayed and felt the arrest was wrong, he refused to sign the famous open letter to Castro in which sixty international renowned figures, including his colleague Plinio Apuleyo Mendoza, condemned the arrest and the Stalin-style humiliating "confession" Padilla was forced to make upon his release. The critic Michael Bell notes, "This attitude has cost [García Márquez's] friendships and has an important bearing on his fundamental sense of politics, and of human solidarity, as manifest in his fiction" (8). García Márquez defended his position to Mendoza: "My view is that although the Revolution took a difficult and sometimes contradictory course after the initial stormy upheavals, it still offers the prospect of a social order

which is more democratic, more just and more suited to our needs"
(*Guava* 99). He also elaborated to Guibert on his decision not to sign the
famous letter:

> What I believe to be really grave is that we intellectuals tend
> to protest and react only when we are personally affected, but
> to do nothing when the same thing happens to a fisherman
> or a priest. What we ought to do is look at the revolution as
> an integral phenomenon, and see how the positive aspects
> infinitely outweigh the negatives ones. Of course,
> manifestations such as the Padilla case are extremely
> dangerous, but they are obstacles that it shouldn't be hard to
> surmount ... That is my position and I won't budge from it.
> I'm not prepared to throw in a revolution on the rubbish
> heap every ten years. (332)

Many people have asked García Márquez to run for public offices,
even president, but he has always turned down these requests, preferring
to use his skills as a journalist to address social and political issues.
Though García Márquez is known primarily as a novelist, he began his
career as a journalist, and he has continued to contribute to newspapers
and magazines long after reaching financial independence. In 1974, for
example, he helped create and fund a political magazine, *Alternativa*,
published in Bogotá. This magazine aimed to provide a different kind of
news coverage, particularly during the overthrow of democracy in Chile
in 1973. The magazine ran 257 issues between 1974–1980, with some
stellar examples of journalism appearing in its pages. As a journalist,
García Márquez has reported on the struggles of Chile, the liberation of
Angola from Portuguese rule, and the situation of Vietnam. In 1977 he
published *Operación Carlota*, a series of essays on Cuba's participation in
the Angolan Revolution. Turning to journalism instead of fiction to deal
directly with political and social issues, García Márquez rejects social-
protest literature, believing it limits artistic expression and freedom. Yet
nearly all of his work, including fiction, addresses social-political
concerns in some way—though often subtly.

Over the years, García Márquez has worked widely for human rights.
In 1974, he served on the Russell Tribunal, a group that investigated the
abuse of human rights in Latin America. In 1978, he founded *Habeas*, a

human rights organization in Mexico City that works to correct the abuses of Latin American authorities and to free political prisoners.

García Márquez has socialized with a wide variety of well-known people, many of them in political arenas, including the former French president François Mitterrand, the Cuban Prime Minister Fidel Castro (with whom he claims to discuss such topics as seafood and literature), the former president of Panama Omar Torrijos, and many famous writers, including the poet Chilean Pablo Neruda, the British writer Graham Greene, and later, the American novelist William Styron. He has often relied upon these friendships to further political causes and has also played an active role as interlocutor between opposing groups.

For example, in 1978, García Márquez accompanied Graham Greene to Washington to act as negotiators of the Panama Canal Treaty. García Márquez participated in various ways in the campaigning of President Omar Torrijos of Panama to have the canal placed under Panamanian sovereignty. He also worked with Graham Green to secure the release of two British bankers who were kidnapped by Salvadorian guerrillas in 1979. And despite his close friendship with Castro, García Márquez has worked to release political prisoners in Cuba, including the 1982 release of the poet Armando Valladares, who had been in prison since 1960.

His other political activities include aiding the Sandinista guerillas in the struggle against the forty-year-old Somoza tyranny in Nicaragua, and supporting the Nicaraguan Revolution in defense against the hostility of the United States In addition, he has served as an intermediary between the Colombian government and guerrilla factions.

In 1980, García Márquez began writing columns dealing with such subjects as the "disappearances" of intellectuals under the Argentine military regime, articles that were syndicated in a couple of dozen Latin American newspapers and magazines. According to Bell-Villada, "These little essays were to provide some of the liveliest, wisest, most distinctly personal magazine reading in Spanish for three consecutive years" (59).

In 1981, García Márquez was awarded the prestigious French Legion of Honor, presented to him by François Mitterrand, whose inauguration García Márquez attended. That same year, García Márquez broke his literary silence with the publication of the highly-acclaimed short novel, *Crónica de una muerta anunciada (Chronicle of a Death Foretold)*. Two-million copies were printed in Columbia,

Argentina, Spain, and Mexico. Despite his hopeful vow, the book was published when Chile's General Pinochet was still in power.

When the book was published, García Márquez was living in Colombia; however, he soon returned to Mexico, requesting political asylum. The Colombian government claimed that García Márquez had simply wanted to create a spectacle in order to gain more publicity for his new book. However, García Márquez argued that the Colombian government had tried to get several M-19 guerrillas to "confess" that García Márquez was one of their sources of funding, and this accusation was his primary reason for leaving. Believing he was being framed by the government, he even tried to sue the military for abuse of authority. Furthermore, the Colombian government was rumored to begin a campaign of repression of the Liberals, with lists of thousands of leftist intellectuals marked for arrest, including García Márquez. If the repressive climate of Chile served as any indicator, then it was imperative for García Márquez to go where he felt safe. After all, in Chile, Pinochet's regime had detained, tortured, and murdered many left-wing artists and intellectuals. The dictatorship had targeted the famous poet and Nobel Laureate, Pablo Neruda, but he died from a stroke before action was taken against him.

For García Márquez, his fame and journalism have provided a platform from which he can support human rights and fight against human injustices. His fiction, journalism, and political beliefs are intertwined, and all influenced by his personal experiences. In Stephen Minta's opinion,

> The years between childhood in Aracataca and the experience of the Cuban revolution were the truly formative ones for García Márquez's career, and much that he has done since that time has followed a relatively logical direction. The main areas of concern, literature, journalism, human rights, and socialist politics, have remained, and his success as a novelist has enabled him to devote considerable amounts of time and money to the pursuit of all of them. (62)

NOBEL PEACE PRIZE

In an interview with the *Paris Review* in 1981, García Márquez stated, "I was asked the other day if I would be interested in the Nobel Prize, but

I think that for me it would be an absolute catastrophe. I would certainly be interested in deserving it, but to receive it would be terrible. I would just complicate even more of the problems of fame" (Stone 339).

A year later, García Márquez was shocked to learn that he had won the Nobel Prize. Most people assumed the next Latin American literary Nobel would go to Octavio Paz, the Mexican poet and essayist. Instead, García Márquez, at fifty-five years old, became the youngest laureate since Albert Camus. He was also the first Colombian and the fourth Latin American to receive this tremendous honor. Years earlier he had claimed that if he ever won the Nobel Prize, he would refuse the award because the Nobel Prize had "become an international lizard hunt" (Rodman 130), but when he actually won, he immediately accepted the international award with honor.

Delighted that the international world recognized the genius of their beloved writer, Colombia celebrated for days with festivities and an outpouring of public sentiment in support of García Márquez. In Mexico, celebrations also ensued. For instance, an entire elementary school showed up at his house in El Pedregal and congratulated him. Though García Márquez still considered himself in exile (and would remain so until 1983), Colombia's president, President Belisario Betancur, personally saw him off to the award ceremony in Stockholm, along with an entourage of sixty performers from six different Colombian dance and musical ensembles. At the ceremony in Sweden, García Márquez, who abhors formality, did not wear a coat and tie, but instead donned a traditional white linen suit of the Caribbean. The prize committee acknowledged García Márquez for his global readership and humanitarianism, the official citation asserting that he has "confirmed his position as a rare storyteller, richly endowed with material, from imagination and experience, which seems inexhaustible." At the ceremony, García Márquez overcame his fear of public speaking and gave a stirring acceptance speech about the political troubles, terrors, and human rights violations in Latin America over the past decade. After the ceremony, there was a party in Stockholm, for which Fidel Castro reportedly provided a large consignment of rum, and "it was the most festive such ceremony [in Stockholm] in nearly a century" (Bell-Villada 60).

With his prize money, García Márquez hoped to launch a new newspaper in Colombia, called *El Otro* (*The Other One*); however, the project never fully succeeded, and eventually the idea was abandoned. Although García Márquez had started to work on a new book of fiction, what he was calling a love story, his status as a Nobel prize winner provided him with little time to write. Winning the Nobel brought more obligations, reporters, and eager fans to his door. Although García Márquez has used his popularity to his advantage in order to promote political and social issues, he also seems uneasy about the trappings of fame. His wife, Mercedes, and his agent both try to protect him from the entourage of journalists, students, and fans who seek him out.

Often described as a shy man, García Márquez dislikes public speaking, and to some may give the impression of being reclusive. However, the few reporters who have conducted long interviews with him usually find him to be warm, friendly, and relaxed. Selden Rodman aptly described his meeting with García Márquez: "I wasn't finding him either shy or detestable, but *muy simpatico*, with a sense of humor that complemented my own. He is a very short man—perhaps five feet five— and a little on the pudgy side, with very white skin. Clearly he doesn't get much exercise or sun. His black hair and moustache are thick and frizzy. He has a way of looking at you sideways when he's about to say something witty, the look of a small boy who delights to shock" (130). He is well-known for his resistance to reporters, however, as he told one reporter: "Look, I've got absolutely nothing against journalists. I've done the job myself and I know what it's like. But if at this stage in my life I were to answer all the questions they want to ask me, I shouldn't be able to work. Besides, I should also be left with nothing to say" (Guibert 308). Though he speaks English well (in addition to Italian and French), he usually conducts the interviews in Spanish, using translators for the reporter, if necessary. Regarding his status as a famous writer, García Márquez once said, "I don't really like to say this because it never sounds sincere, but I would really have liked for my books to be published after my death, so I wouldn't have to go through all this business of fame and being a great writer" (Stone 337).

Though García Márquez now earns enough from his fiction to not have to work, he remains aware of the troubles money can bring. "I have a profound belief in the power of money to corrupt. If a writer, particular at the start of his career, is given an award or grant ... he is to some extent compromised" (Guibert 333).

Although García Márquez associates with many famous politicians and writers, he continues to remain loyal to his family and friends. In interviews, he often refers to Mercedes, always speaking of her with affection and tenderness, and shows similar affection toward his friends: "I don't break or cut myself off from my old friends, and they're the ones who bring me back to earth; they always keep their feet on the ground and they're not famous" (Stone 328). As much as García Márquez is involved in grave politics, he also likes festivity. However, he has never liked ceremonies, and much prefers to spend time with his friends in a relaxed environment. Furthermore, he does not want to lock himself up in an ivory tower. Though he acknowledges a writer needs solitude to work, he also recognizes the danger of removing oneself from society and has written about this extensively. The theme of solitude and its potential destruction appears in nearly all of his work. In fact, in the words of García Márquez, the downfall of Macondo "comes from this lack of solidarity—the solitude which results when everyone is acting for himself alone" (Guibert 314).

He also understands the perils of his fame, and even with his oldest, dearest friends, he is now more careful about what he says and does. For example, he no longer writes personal letters. After he found out someone sold some of his personal letters to the archives of a U.S. university, he stopped writing to anyone: "The discovery that my letters too were a saleable commodity made me incredibly depressed and I never wrote another one after that" (*Guava* 120). Instead, to remain in contact with close friends, he spends a good deal of time on the phone, or "I go half way round the world at some insane cost to see them" (*Guava* 120).

AFTER THE NOBEL

After winning the Nobel prize, García Márquez found himself obligated to participate in many public events, and was not able to continue writing the love story he had started until late 1983. To immerse himself in his work, he moved to Cartagena, Colombia, where his parents were living. When he discusses his family in interviews, García Márquez speaks about his grandparents, wife, and children with intimacy and affection. But, perhaps because he did not meet his parents until he was five or six years old and never lived for a long period of time with them, his relationship with his parents appears to be more distant. He has described his relationship with his mother as "serious," but on good terms: "I believe there's nothing she and I can't tell each other and no subject we can't talk about, but we've always treated each other with a certain almost professional formality, rather than any intimacy" (19). However, even as an adult, he did not seem to know his father well—he has said little about him or their relationship, except to point out the differences between his father and his grandfather: "My father was not only unlike my grandfather, he was almost the exact opposite. His personality, his idea of authority, his whole view of the world and of his relationship with his children, were completely different" (*Guava* 21). However, one of García Márquez's distant cousins remembered, "His father believed in him a great deal. He used to tell his relatives that Gabito was a genius, but people didn't believe him. He used to say that Gabito had two brains" (Paternostro, section I).

Living in Colombia again, García Márquez returned to his writing routine, spending eight hours a day on the novel. Within a year, having accomplished quite a bit of writing, he returned to his home in Mexico City to continue working on the novel. Nothing about his writing routines or habits changed much over the years. For example, a superstitious man, García Márquez always likes to have yellow roses in a vase on his desk while he works. One aspect however did change: for the first time, he switched from using an electric typewriter to a computer. When he finished the book in 1985, he arrived in Barcelona, the home of his literary agent, and instead of carrying the bundled manuscript, he wore three diskettes around his neck.

On December 5, 1985, a million copies of *Love in the Time of Cholera* were released in the four most populous Spanish-speaking countries. This book, one of his most popular, is a love story based on his parents' courtship. Inspired by an image of two old people dancing a bolero on the deck of a boat, the novel depicts the love between the two characters that finally burgeons when they are close to eighty-years old. One of his most straight-forward and accessible narratives, it also is as rich and artistic as his other works, and received prominent critical praise in Latin America, Europe, and the United States—in the latter, most notably with an enthusiastic review by the recluse novelist Thomas Pynchon in the *The New York Times Book Review*.

In America, García Márquez has been well received, to say the least. His work has influenced such highly acclaimed American authors as John Barth, Anne Tyler, and fellow Nobel Laureate, Toni Morrison. When *One Hundred Years of Solitude* first appeared in America, it was something new and wholly different. Bell-Villada elaborates: "Breaking from the claustrophobic atmosphere that had permeated French and American writing, García Márquez reopened the doors and windows and took on the life of the streets, giving us a vast panorama in which every grand historical situation—from utopian harmony and dizzy prosperity to flaccid decadence and class war—was fully conjured up" (10). American reviews of his work are typically positive, and a large amount of scholarly and critical studies have emerged in the last decade. Of his American audience, he says, "They are professional readers ... some are progressive, others so reactionary, as they are supposed to be; but as readers, they are wonderful" (Guibert 306). García Márquez has always held mixed views of the United States. He praises the country's colleges, journalism, and films, and also admires the wealth of literary criticism. However, he often openly condemns the United State's international policies, and is vehemently critical of the United States's role in Colombian history.

Later Years

In the 1980s, the rise in the narcotic drug trade brought a dangerous wave of violence to Colombia. By the mid-eighties, much of county had slid into mayhem and violence. Narcotic trafficking emerged as Colombia's most dominant economic force, with the majority of the exported drugs going to the United States To this day, Colombia is the world's major producer of cocaine. The powerful drug kingpins were famous for intimidating, murdering, or torturing anyone who tried to defeat them, including journalists, politicians, and law enforcement officers. Kidnappings became a popular tactic, threatening both citizens and foreigners. In addition to the violence of the drug trade, several guerrilla groups also emerged during the '80s, adding to the chaos and violence of the nation. The critic Bell-Villada describes this troubled atmosphere:

> The 1980s have seen the emergence of a new phase of violence, a complex struggle involving the half-dozen guerilla groups (nationalist as much as Marxist), the right-wing paramilitary squads, the enormously rich *narcotraficatnes* and their private troops, and the national army and police themselves, who routinely make their presence felt and their

automatic weapons visible on the city streets and rural
highways. The government, though formally a liberal
democracy, can show fast and furious repression, as in the
1979 arrest orders for a thousand individuals, many of them
prominent artists and intellectuals. (28)

The danger continues into the present day. For example, in 1999,
nearly two hundred people were kidnapped every month. Because of
Colombia's volatile climate and wide-spread violence, García Márquez
spends most of his time at his permanent residence in Mexico City with
Mercedes. His son Rodrigo now lives in the United States; and his other
son, Gonzalo, is a graphic designer in Mexico City. García Márquez also
owns residencies in Cartagena, Barranquilla, Bogotá, and Cuernavaca in
Colombia, as well as Paris and Barcelona. His homes are each furnished
the same way, with white carpets, modern art, an expensive sound
system, and a Macintosh computer. Unlike his earlier days, he now owns
an impressive library. Whenever García Márquez stays at his place in
Colombia, he travels in a bulletproof sedan with several secret-service
agents because of the high rate of violence.

Throughout the eighties and nineties, García Márquez devoted his
energy to writing, teaching, and political activism. On several occasions,
he acted as a mediator between the Colombian government and leftist
guerrilla groups. Always involved with politics and social issues, he
continued working in favor of peace, disarmament, and human rights.
For example, in 1986, he gave a powerful speech in Mexico against world
armament before the Group of Six (Mexico, Argentina, Greece, Sweden,
India, and Tanzania). García Márquez's views carry immense weight in
Latin America—he is one of the few who has won the trust of both the
governments and revolutionaries. Furthermore, he has also quietly used
his friendship with Castro to release a number of political prisoners over
the years.

In addition to his dedication to politics, he also began to commit
himself more closely to the medium of film. In the 1980s, he undertook
teaching at a film school in Havana, organizing and directing the
Foundation of New Latin American Cinema. García Márquez has
expressed interest in film since he first began reviewing films at the *El
Espectador*. He has written many film scripts throughout the years,
including *Viva Sandino*, a screenplay about the revolution in Nicaragua.

He has also translated and written subtitles and written screenplays for television. Furthermore, several of his own works, mainly the short stories, have been turned into films. While most of these were shot in Spanish in Latin America, there is also a version of *Chronicle of a Death Foretold* in Italian (1987). The most recent film is the Mexican adaptation of *No One Writes to the Colonel* (1999). Several works of fiction were also adapted for the stage, including *Chronicle of a Death Foretold* in New York (1990). For a time, there was talk of *Autumn of the Patriarch* being adapted to the screen, starring Marlon Brando and directed by Sean Penn; however, this project appears to be on hold. Though he admires the power of film, García Márquez has also expressed ambivalence about the adaptation of his fiction. For example, he does not want *One Hundred Years of Solitude* to be turned into a film, stating, "I prefer that it remain a private relationship between the reader and the book" (Stone 338). To discourage offers, in 1981, his agent raised the asking price to three million dollars.

In the 1990s, García Márquez published several highly acclaimed works of fiction and nonfiction. The novel *El general en su labertino* (*The General in His Labyrinth*), based on the life of Simón Bolívar, was published in 1990. Before he began writing this novel, he read histories of the life of Bolívar, who was known as The Liberator for leading the uprising against Spain and capturing Colombian independence in 1819.

In 1992, *Strange Pilgrims*, a collection of stories, was published, and in 1994, he published another work of fiction, *Love and Other Demons*. This was followed in 1996 with a work of journalism detailing the atrocities of the Colombian drug trade, *News of a Kidnapping*. The book describes the kidnapping of ten people, mostly journalists, by a Colombian drug cartel; one of the victims included a friend of García Márquez. Clearly, García Márquez has never abandoned his love for journalism. In 1994, he founded the Foundation for a New Latin American Journalism, which has a school in Cartagena, Colombia and sponsors workshops and scholarships throughout Latin America. In 1999, he purchased a struggling Colombian news magazine, *Cambio*, with his Nobel Prize money. Today, the magazine continues to thrive.

García Márquez has never stopped speaking out in regards to politics. He maintains his controversial friendship with Castro, and in 1998 was a guest of Castro for the historic visit of Pope John Paul II to Cuba. He also added President Clinton to his long list of close and powerful friends. On his campaign, Clinton had called *One Hundred Years of Solitude* one of his favorite books. At first, García Márquez thought he was just trying to win the Latin vote, but later, he had the opportunity to meet Clinton, and found him to be genuine and friendly. During Clinton's second term, García Márquez wrote a defense of President Clinton in the Monica Lewinsky scandal, comparing the United States former president to the persecuted Hester Prynne in Nathaniel Hawthorne's *The Scarlet Letter*, an article that appeared in *Cambio* and was reprinted on Salon.com. Though García Márquez helped to establish better relations between Colombia and the United States, and Clinton was a good friend, he was also not afraid to challenge Clinton's policies. For example, speaking out on another political scandal during this time period, García Márquez wrote an editorial for the the *New York Times* in a plea to consider the mental stability for the six-year-old "refugee" Elián González, and argued for the boy to be returned to his father in Cuba. Throughout the nineties, García Márquez wrote articles for a variety of newspapers, relying on journalism to approach political issues.

García Márquez's life changed in 1999 when was diagnosed with lymphatic cancer. He underwent chemotherapy, spending much of his time at clinics in Los Angeles, where his son, filmmaker Rodrigo Garcia, lives (García Márquez's travel restriction to the United States had finally been lifted). After the initial treatments, García Márquez cloistered himself off in his home in Mexico City, much like he did when he wrote *One Hundred Years of Solitude*. "I reduced relations with my friends to a minimum, disconnected the telephone, cancelled the trips and all sorts of current and future plans," he said. "And I locked myself in to write every day, without interruption" (Forero 1). He scaled back on his journalism and political involvement to recall his childhood years.

This time, García Márquez was not working on fiction, but researching and writing his memoirs—promising a set of three volumes. He spoke with relatives, conducting numerous interviews with them, and tried once again to recreate Aracataca. The first volume recounts the years of his childhood up until he published *Leaf Storm* and left for Europe as a correspondent. The second volume will conclude with the publication of *One Hundred Years of Solitude*. The third volume will encompass the years up until the present, focusing on his friendships with world leaders.

The first volume *Viver para contarla*, (*Living to Tell the Tale*) was published in 2001, selling out its first print run in Latin America and Spain. The 579-page book quickly became the best selling book ever in the Spanish-speaking world. It is the fastest selling book in the history of Latin American publishing, even selling faster than *One Hundred Years of Solitude*.

In January 2003, the publishing house Knopf released the memoir in the United States. In a bold move, Knopf distributed the book in Spanish—the book became the first foreign-language book any major American imprint has published without an accompanying English translation. Thousands of U.S. residents purchased the Spanish version of *Living to Tell the Tale*—it sold out of its first printing of 50,000 copies. Mostly, the news of the book reached people in the U.S. by word of mouth—García Márquez did not go on a book tour or agree to interviews to garner publicity.

In March 2003, García Márquez turned seventy-five years old. Recovered from his treatments, he has been seen out and about, dancing with Mercedes at parties late into the night. He declines to speak of his illness. According to Francisco Goldman in the the *New York Times Magazine*, in addition to finishing his memoirs, García Márquez is also said to be writing a new novel.

Though he has spent most of the last few years writing and recovering, he continues to speak out on political issues. For example, in April 2003, Fidel Castro stirred up international controversy when he jailed seventy-five dissidents for terms of up to twenty-eight years and executed three hijackers. Many artists, journalists, and intellectuals condemned the arrests. However, a month later, 160 writers, actors, and artists from across the Americas and Europe signed a declaration in support of the Cuban Government. García Márquez signed the letter, which supports Cuba's national sovereignty but does not specifically express support for Castro's policies. García Márquez also made it understood that he condemned use of the death penalty. However, similar to his reaction to the Herberto Padilla controversy back in 1971, García Márquez did not criticize the Cuban government and still has not given up on the success of the Revolution. Consequently, García Márquez's friendship with Castro has been the cause of much controversy. Though García Márquez is well-respected for his role in acting as a intermediary between governments and revolutionaries, he is often criticized in Latin American for becoming too easily enchanted by men in power. Others close to the author claim that García Márquez recognizes and repudiates Castro's human right violations, but remains loyal to him out of friendship.

In November 2003, Knopf released the English translation of his memoir *Living to Tell the Tale*. In the public eye once again, this time for his literature instead of his politics, García Márquez continues to receive wide, honorable recognition and praise. In New York City, renowned literary figures honored his life-long achievements in a literary tribute. Speakers included Salman Rushdie, Paul Auster, William Kennedy, and Edwidge Danticat, along with a video message from President Clinton.

García Márquez is one of the most famous and admired living writers in the world today. Certainly, most Latin Americans know who he is, and more than likely, have read something by him, whether a novel or a newspaper column. The critic Bell-Villada attests, "Because of the enormous reach of his reputation, García Márquez is now seen not just as another major author but as the prime symbol of the surge of creativity in Latin American letters in our time" (203). García Márquez, recognizing that he has affected the reading public, specifically Latin Americans, gave his opinion on the role of literature and politics: "I don't think literature should be used as a firearm. But, even against your own will, your ideological positions are inevitably reflected in your writing and they influence readers. I think my books have had political impact in Latin America because they help to create a Latin American identity; they help Latin Americans to become more aware of their own culture" (Simons 131). His fame and prestige grow larger with every passing year. His best known book, *One Hundred Years of Solitude*, has been translated into over thirty languages, and sold millions of copies in United States alone. His reputation and fame have extended far past the borders of Latin America; today Gabriel García Márquez is one of the most widely read and respected authors in the international community.

WORKS CITED

Bell, Michael. *Gabriel García Márquez: Solitude and Solidarity*. New York: St. Martin's Press, 1993.
Bell-Villada, Gene H. *García Márquez: The Man and His Work*. Chapel Hill: The University of North Carolina Press, 1990.

Donoso, José. *The Boom in Spanish American Literature: A Personal History.* Trans. Gregory Kolovakos. New York: Columbia University Press, 1977.

Forero, Juan. "García Márquez, Fighting Cancer, Issues Memoirs." *New York Times*, 9 October 2002. 3 pages. TheModernWord.com, (4 November 2003). <*www.themodernword.com/gabo/gabo_nyt_memoirs.html.*

García Márquez, Gabriel. "Gabriel García Márquez Meets Ernest Hemingway." Trans. Randolph Hogan. *New York Times.* 26 July 1981: 4 pages. (4 November 2003). <*www.nytimes.com/books/97/06/15/reviews/marquez-hemingway.html*>.

———. "The Challenge." *The New Yorker.* 6 October 2003: 100–105.

García Márquez, Gabriel and Plinio Apuleyo Mendoza. *The Fragrance of Guava.* Trans. Ann Wright. London: Versco, 1983.

Goldman, Francisco. "In the Shadow of the Patriarch." *New York Times Magazine.* 2 November 2003: 38+.

Guibert, Rita. "Gabriel García Márquez." *Seven Voices: Seven Latin American Writers Talk to Rita Guibert.* Trans. Frances Partridge. New York: Knopf, 1973. 305–337.

Janes, Regina. *Gabriel García Márquez: Revolution in Wonderland.* Columbia: University of Missouri Press, 1981.

Mellen, Joan, ed. *Literary Masters: Gabriel García Márquez.* Vol. 5. Detroit: Gale Group, 2000.

Minta, Stephen. *Gabriel García Márquez: Writer of Colombia.* London: Jonathan Cape, 1987.

Paternostro, Silvana. "Solitude and Company: An Oral Biography of Gabriel García Márquez." *Paris Review*, Issue 166 (Summer 2003): 10 pages. (4 November 2003). < *www.parisreview.com/tpr166/solitude.html*>.

Rodman, Selden. "Gabriel García Márquez." *Tongues of Fallen Angels: Conversations.* New York: New Directions, 1974. 113–133.

Simons, Marlise. "Gabriel García Márquez on Love, Plagues and Politics." *New York Times*, 21 February 1988. Reprinted in *Literary Masters: Gabriel García Márquez.* Vol. 5. Mellen, Joan, ed. Detroit: Gale Group, 2000.

Stone, Peter. "Gabriel García Márquez" in *Writers At Work: The Paris Review Interviews—Sixth Series.* George Plimpton, ed. New York: Viking, 1984. 313–339.

Vargas Llosa, Mario. "García Márquez: From Aracataca to Macondo" in *Modern Critical Views: Gabriel García Márquez.* Harold Bloom, ed. New York: Chelsea House Publishers, 1989. 5–19.

GRACE KIM

Nothing Interesting Has Happened to Me: The Works of Gabriel García Márquez

In a statement that seems stolen from the narrator of *One Hundred Years of Solitude*, Gabriel García Márquez once remarked that since the age of eight and the death of his maternal grandfather, to whom he attributes his literary genius, "nothing interesting has happened to me." In this way we may enter into the world of García Márquez, to whom it seems possible to evoke the trajectory of a life and world from a single event, a sentiment, or even a name, as we see in his celebrated account of seven generations of Buendías, who call all their males either José Arcadio or Aureliano in a manner at once scripted and bewilderingly incidental. The matriarch of the clan, Úrsula Iguarán, who outlives most of her line and whose eventual total blindness produces a clarity of vision regarding generations of her children's daily destinies, never succeeds in altering even a step of her family's determined misfortune of incest, solitude and monstrous decrepitude. The triple theme that sustains *One Hundred Years*, which evokes the culmination of García Márquez's art, is as relevant to the casual reader as it is the literary critic and as important to the individual as it is to a global millennial community. García Márquez's career delivers a lifetime of deep insight explored and developed through decades of personal and professional growth. The consistency of his characterization and essentially anecdotal style is underscored by the range of his narrative structure and tone, which varies from the prolonged and funereal chapters in *The Autumn of the Patriarch* to the universally accessible romance in *Love in the Time of Cholera*. The family epic of *One Hundred of Years of Solitude* falls somewhat between *Autumn* and *Love* in tone and narrative structure; it is a work of necessary and inevitable ambivalences to celebrate without regret the most extreme and startling conditions of life.

The fearful fascination with incest precedes the start of the narrative but it is the true origin of the story of "races condemned to one hundred years of solitude." Úrsula, worried that her marriage to her cousin, José Arcadio Buendía, will result in an offspring born with the tail of a pig, refuses to consummate the marriage and inadvertently causes the murder of a man who compromises her husband's honor by publicly ridiculing his virility after an unfortunate cockfight. José Arcadio Buendía kills the man but feels so much empathy for the ghost of his rival that he decides to leave town to respect the ghost's sorrow. The foundation of García Márquez's most famous fiction, then, lies in the incest taboo, which successfully haunts the Buendías to the end of their line seven generations later.

In fact to submit to criticism a casual plot summary of this novel is the most unjust and aesthetically pernicious act against Macondo, the fictional village made as real by García Márquez as Faulkner's imaginary Yoknapatawpha County, because it is only the authority of the properly invested narrator who may carry the full burden of Úrsula's generations. The author's style, whose origin he traces to the storytelling of his maternal grandmother, comprises the infrastructure of his novels so that the tone set in the first sentences of *One Hundred Years* or his more explicitly literary *The Autumn of the Patriarch* affects not only the introduction, but also the climax, denouement and final collapse of the novel's fiction and fictional structure. Like Úrsula, whose long life convinces her that time moves continually in circles, the reader of García Márquez learns to appreciate the cyclical outrages demonstrated with consistent ease by a skilled narrator who always knows more curiosity and outrage than the listener at every point of his tale, orienting the reader in an exhilarating disorientation from the first word to the last. For although we are always aware that we are being told a tale, one that is local and sealed in a regional narcissism of community, progress, and finally, decrepitude, the fiction of García Márquez sustains a unique and serious interaction with the realities of late colonial and post-colonial history and culture in the Americas so that the so-called magic realism of his craft is no mere literary device but rather a stunning demonstration of one man's communion with the riches of his personal memory and national history.

Mario Vargas Llosa, novelist and biographer of García Márquez, attributes the enormity of his influence to the "total" nature of his art, which submits itself not only to literary and artistic rigor, but also to socio-political insight and relevance. Of the "total" novel of García Márquez, Vargas Llosa describes it as of "one of those insanely ambitious creations which aspire to compete with reality on an equal basis, confronting it with an image and qualitatively matching it in vitality, vastness, and complexity." In the world created by García Márquez, one idea creates a universe over and over again. The idea is most simply time, but time is never quite so simple in García Márquez's imagination. Time stops and starts, reverses and goes on forever so that dictators live some unknowable age "between" 107 and 232 years in *The Autumn of the Patriarch*, and a gypsy conjurer regains his lost youth with a set of false teeth, which deny the decades of age and illness that have underscored his decrepitude for a generation. Time seems to occur in an instant, as in a volume of book that contains within its two covers endless years of truth. For García Márquez, time and fate are incorrigibly linked so that once time is begun, whether at the founding of a village or the opening of a story, the end is already known, prescribed and inevitable. This motif is most directly explored in the novella *Chronicle of a Death Foretold*, in which the intention to kill Santiago Nasar becomes known to the village in the course of an early morning but no one does anything to stop the tragedy. The twins, Pablo and Pedro Vicario, have broadcast their vengeance expecting that someone will do them the favor of stopping the killing, which is a matter of honor and not real passion. However, as Pablo Vicario tells the narrator: "There's no way out of this. It's as if it had already happened."

The notion that events are predetermined and unalterable underlies the author's manipulation of names and naming, memory and the search for origins throughout his works. In the last phases of *One Hundred Years*, Úrsula is confused by the behavior of the twins, José Arcadio Segundo and Aureliano Segundo, which reverses the usual characteristics attributed to their ancestral names. Contrary to history, it is the former who is withdrawn and solitary and the latter who is impulsive and ill-fated. Úrsula suspects that the brothers, who played the usual games of twins in their childhood—swapping identities in order to exasperate their family and friends—might have gotten themselves mixed up at some later point of the game and settled into the wrong names for the remainder of their lives. Upon their simultaneous deaths in separate houses, José Arcadio Segundo is accidentally laid at his brother's tombstone, and vice versa because "the sad drunkards who carried them out of the house got the coffins mixed up and buried them in the wrong graves." In this way fate conforms to destiny as if the Buendías were indeed "a machine with unavoidable repetitions, a turning wheel that would have gone on spilling into eternity were it not for the progressive and irremediable wearing of the axle," as the ancient fortune teller to generations of troubled Buendías believes.

No one in the world of García Márquez escapes fate, which is tied up in the histories of a name and the origin of time, so that life is a progressive decrepitude that need only be played out in order to be realized. Yet despite this certainty, García Márquez also depicts characters whose rebellion against fate causes a suspension of time that endures often to the end of life. In his first novel, *Leaf Storm* (1955), García Márquez employs a multi-subjective narration of the suspended burial of a community pariah, who has hung himself in solitude with no one to mourn his death. In this early work, which has often been read in the context of Faulkner's influence, García Márquez narrates the controversial suicide from the varied perspectives of an aged colonel, his daughter and her small son, who bury the man against the wishes of the town who wish to throw the former doctor to the vultures for his earlier sins against the community. *Leaf Storm*, whose style has more to do with the later *The Autumn of the Patriarch* than *One Hundred Years of Solitude*, is a somber and protracted narrative that measures the events of the past through overlapping reminiscences of the three voices to elucidate the present suspension of the town regarding the dead man. The three consciousness recounted in *Leaf Storm* often hinge upon distinct shared moments in the present but diverge into radically different monologues from each coincidence, a technique the novelist seems to abandon after this early work.

In fact, Faulkner's influence is one that García Márquez freely admits, referring to the former as "my master" in his Nobel Prize lecture delivered to the Swedish Academy in December 8, 1982. Among other influences he cites Hemingway, Joyce, Woolf and Kafka, whose *The Metamorphosis* evidently made a tremendous impact on the young Gabriel. He remembers his introduction to Kafka as his first inspiration to write fiction:

> One night a friend [at the university] lent me a book of short stories by Franz Kafka. I went back to the pension where I was staying and began to read *The Metamorphosis*. The first line almost knocked me off the bed ... I didn't know anyone was allowed to write things like that. If I had known, I would have started writing a long time ago. So I immediately started writing short stories.

Despite what he calls his "apprenticeship" under the masters of the modern novel, his voice in *One Hundred Years of Solitude* is most distinctly his own. The outrageousness of his humor is always detectable though in varying degrees throughout his work—less sharp in *Love in the Time of Cholera* and infinitely dark in *The Autumn of the Patriarch*. Garcia Márquez honors all aspects of life and death, though with unpredictable feeling, as he does not always reserve special reverence for what we know to be the solemnities of life nor does he moralize upon the weaknesses of his characters, which simply exist as fictional assumptions because of their true reference to life. The realities of life, which often seems blurred and discounted in the enchanted life of the Buendías or the surreal palace of the patriarch, comprise the heart of García Márquez's fiction. Of the eccentric and often whimsical nature of his work, he has said: "The trouble is that many people believe that I'm a writer of fantastic fiction, when actually I'm a very realistic person and write what I believe is the true socialist realism."

The "socialist realism" to which he refers is often a provocative issue for much of his readership, which spans the globe but must has special import in North and South America, where much of his fiction takes place. Certainly, García Márquez's political presence in the Americas has both complicated and enriched his literary eminence. After 1960, when he lived in Havana for six months working for the Cuban news agency Prensa Latina, the United States government denied the novelist entrance to the country. In 1971, when he was conferred an honorary doctorate from Columbia University, the government issued a provisional visa that required an official invitation for the Colombian to enter the country. In 1984, when he was invited to attend a discussion of U.S. policies in Central America, he was still under prohibition and permitted only the provisional visa offered him in earlier times. Despite these political restrictions, García Márquez praised his U.S. audience in a 1973 interview as "professional readers ... as readers, they're wonderful."

Despite García Márquez's abjuration of the political novel, which he seems to implicate in the category of "bad literature" and detrimental to the progress of socialism, his politics and his experiences of the politics of his times are nowhere completely absent from his works. Regina Janes traces his politics in her essay *"Liberals, Conservatives, and Bananas: Colombian Politics in the Fictions of Gabriel García Márquez,"* which begins with the author's statement that readers of his most famous novel who are unfamiliar with the history of his country might appreciate the novel as a good novel but would miss much of the significance embedded in the details of the story. So it is the case that many thoughtful critics, while acknowledging the author's stated distaste for the political novel, interpret the political aspect of García Márquez's work as a central component of his art. Oftentimes, as in the case of Janes, critics knowledgeable in the history of Latin America and particularly Colombia must illuminate for (English-speaking) readers, who experience García Márquez only through translation, the extra-literary signifiers in his prose. A great portion of García Márquez's readership, who encounters his voice only through the mediation of a translator, may not need to understand the author's country to enjoy his voice. Still we must be remiss to completely deny the gaps in signification not only in the view of politics but also of culture and language, which exist in any expressive exchange for better and for worse. It is a paradox worthy of García Márquez that his work offers community and global interpretation even as it does so through the aesthetic expression of solitude and spiritual decay.

* *

When *Cien años de soledad* (*One Hundred Years of Solitude*) was published in 1967, the decade in which Latin America and thereafter the world experienced what came to be called The Boom in the novel, García Márquez was an unknown journalist who had several books published, but never more than seven hundred copies per book. *Cien años de soledad* sold out its first printing of eight thousand copies within a week in the single city of Buenos Aires and launched an overnight celebrity for its author; at one point new editions were churned out at a rate of one per week to satisfy the public's demand. By the late 1990s, *Cien años de soledad* could be read in thirty different languages and had sold over twenty million copies. A veritable icon in his native Colombia, García Márquez clearly ranks as one of the few novelists in this or any time that has enjoyed both critical and popular success.

Vargas Llosa's commentary on the ambition of García Márquez's fiction is particularly instructive in the case of this novel, which introduces Macondo as a world "so recent that many things lacked names, and in order to indicate them it was necessary to point." The relatively virgin world of the Buendías, then, is so new that the progressive discoveries of Macondo's founding family, its efforts to name and inhabit this world, is a kind of Genesis. In a town where everyone is under the age of thirty and no one has yet to die, the evidence of the outside world via the annual arrival of gypsies bearing miracles of science (among others, a magnifying glass and a magnet) inspires a devastating awe in the innocence of the certain fated males of the line, who, ultimately frustrated in their search for an absolute future in line with the revelations, sacrifice the passage of time in their singular nostalgia for the past wherein lies the origin of their consciousness. That burden of memory seems to be the hereditary ailment of the Buendía patriarchy, whose members compulsively locate the beginning and end of themselves in a single memory after which time no longer moves. These memories are always fragments of an experience that is interpreted by the character in a manner that is often unique, perverse and highly sensual. García Márquez, in these events, isolates a single datum of sensual experience that the character carries with him for the remainder of his life like a repressed trauma or fatal obsession.

For García Márquez, solitude is like a disease that preoccupies an individual and quarantines him from society forever. The solitary character becomes lost in his memories, desires or illusions until he loses everything, even memory itself. For instance, the colonel Aureliano Buendía remembers for the rest of his life the afternoon that his father took him to discover ice, which he is startled to find is "boiling" upon first touch; he remembers it and nothing else at the climax of his life as he stands in front of a firing squad whose execution is never fulfilled. In earlier instances, his father, José Arcadio Buendía forsakes the world chasing after the novelties of his world. As many times as an idea occurs to José Arcadio, the extremes of his imagination carries him off in an impenetrable fervor that disregards all else but the pursuit of that single idea: the revelation of alchemy becomes José Arcadio's failure to find the philosopher's stone; the discovery of the pendulum culminates in the ecstatic possibility of a flying time machine; with the daguerreotype he attempts to catch, to prove once and for all, the image of God. José Arcadio never finds God. Instead he meets the reconciling ghost of the man he murdered in a duel in his youth and discovers after a pang of nostalgia that time has ceased to progress for him:

> … he went into Aureliano's workshop and asked him: "What day is today?" Aureliano told him it was Tuesday. "I was thinking the same thing," José Arcadio Buendía said, "but suddenly I realized that it's still Monday, like yesterday. Look at the sky, look at the walls, look at the begonias. Today is Monday too." Used to his manias, Aureliano paid no attention to him. On the net day, Wednesday, José Arcadio Buendía went back to the workshop. "This is a disaster," he said. "Look at the air, listen to the buzzing of the sun, the same as yesterday and the day before. Today is Monday too." … He spent six hours examining things, trying to find a difference from their appearance on the previous day in the hope of discovering in them some change that would reveal the passage of time…. On Friday, before anyone arose, he watched the appearance of nature again until he did not have the slightest doubt but that it was Monday.

José Arcadio Buendía, shaken by nostalgia and the evidence of death, gives over to the power of his formidable imagination, which convinces him that time has ceased because there is nothing of the progress of life that he can see with certainty in the world. Detained from a sincere attempt to destroy the world starting from his laboratory and extending to the rest of the house, José Arcadio spends the remainder of his days strapped to a chestnut tree in the courtyard of the Buendía estate, mumbling unintelligibly in a language everyone assumes is nonsensical until the local priest is startled to hear Latin from the madman and confirms his slanted lucidity.

José Arcadio's son, the legendary Colonel Aureliano Buendía literally officiates over his solitude with the decree that no one, not even his mother, Úrsula, may enter the circle of chalk drawn around him by an attendant at his every stop. The colonel, separated from the rest of humanity by a radius of ten feet, launches thirty-two unsuccessful wars against the Conservative regime, which he thereafter denounces as the ignoble manifestation of personal pride, which stands among García Márquez's symbols of characterization as a particularly virulent strain of the disease of solitude. When Colonel Aureliano Buendía returns to Macondo detached from all his past he shuts himself up in the old room of solitude and commences the meaningless task of making two gold fishes inset with ruby eyes only to melt them down at the end of each day to replicate the labor the following day.

Ironically, Aureliano silently succeeds in the violence his father meant against the world in his youth and before the wars, when he called the help of twenty men to drag José Arcadio Buendía from his wrecking spree to the chestnut tree. Decades later, the son mentally annihilates everything that his father was not able to touch save the single memory of the afternoon when he was taken to discover the burning ice and the endlessly created and dying golden fishes, which he refuses to sell as he once did when he realizes that people have begun to collect them as a historic relic and not as a piece of jewelry. When Úrsula importunes him to remember the family as they sit one evening at dinner, he replies, "I'm sorry. It's just that the war has done away with everything."

The mother, who often seems to evoke the voice of compassion that García Márquez explicates with greater candidness in press interviews and honorary lectures, becomes the intermediary between her descendents and the reader as she in her old age and blindness redefines her perspective of her progeny. It is Úrsula who identifies the generations-old distinction in the characters of the José Arcadios and Aurelianos and bemoans the cyclical nature of the family's spiritual flaws. Of her firstborn, the famous revolutionary, whose meditative precociousness had startled her from his infancy, she realizes without reproach:

Colonel Aureliano Buendía had not lost his love for the

family because he had been hardened by the war, as she had thought before, but that he had never loved anyone, not even his wife Remedios or the countless one-night women who had passed through his life, and much less his sons. She sensed that he had fought so many wars not out of idealism, as everyone had thought, nor had he renounced a certain victory because of fatigue, as everyone had thought, but that he had won and lost for the same reason, pure and sinful pride. She reached the conclusion that the son for whom she would have given her life was simply a man incapable of love. One night when she was carrying him in her belly she heard him weeping. It was such a definite lament that José Arcadio Buendía woke up beside her and was happy with the idea that his son was going to be a ventriloquist.... But the lucidity of her old age allowed her to see, and she said so many times, that the cries of children in their mothers' wombs are not announcements of ventriloquism or a faculty for prophecy but an unmistakable sign of an incapacity for love.

It is perhaps this voice, combining insight, melancholy and humor, that is closest to that of the author who illuminates Úrsula with the strength of human tenderness to accept the true character of her son. Her realization, which reads like the narrator's private meditation upon a man with whom he is personally acquainted, does not spare the reader the full impact of the ancient and rarefied disillusionment regarding the epic farce of humanity manifest in the loveless son and revolutionary, nor does it leave out the seeming callousness of the father and husband who, in the evident distress of his unborn child, is more interested in the dramatic capacity of his future vocation than his early mark of sorrow. As he did in the narrative structure of his earliest fiction, *Leaf Storm*, and the grammatical structure of *The Autumn*, García Márquez leaps across bounds of perspective and tone with humanity and humor in the narrative of *One Hundred Years*, which incorporates "everything," following Vargas Llosa's remark on the creation of the total novel.

The progressive oeuvre of García Márquez shows an evolution of his narrative skill and development of character. One may become acquainted with the signs and symbols of his art, which overlap from story to story, novel to novel, fiction to reality in a grand mosaic that is consistent for all its multiplicity. For instance, March is always the month of beginnings—the month of the gypsies—while October is always a time of depression, marked by rain and intolerable memories. The smell of almond trees as the bitterness of love, gold cyanide as the fumes of fear and death, and uniforms without insignias as the mark of extreme solitude are all repeated symbols in the works of García Márquez. Characters who appear but once in passing in *One Hundred Years* are pivotal members in the drama of earlier works. The central dramas of *Leaf Storm* and *Love in the Time of Cholera* may be inset into the grand epic of *One Hundred Years*, in which the priest Pup from *Leaf Storm* and the romance of *Love* are incidental elements.

The passion of Fermina Daza and Florentino Ariza in *Love in the Time of Cholera* is the fictionalized account of the author's parents' love, as García Márquez reveals in the first volume of his memoir *Living to Tell the Tale* (2003) as well as in earlier commentaries on this work. The author's memoir, almost as incredible as his fiction, offers a unique opportunity of insight into his art, which he discusses without formality or reservation. The exceptional coherence of his life and his art seems an added tribute to the phenomenon of *One Hundred Years*, which has inspired something of a cult of personality as well as literary fame, particularly in Latin America. The memoir is a propitious addition to García Márquez's oeuvre. One might joke that it is one of the only examples of his writing that recognizes the normal progress of chronology and time, but in actuality, even this cannot escape the craft of a narrative genius whose origins are never at the story's start nor causes in precedent of their effects, as we might usually expect. As he writes in the epigram to this first volume of his memoirs: "Life is not what one lived, but what one remembers and how one remembers it in order to recount it." So that the story of his remembrances begins with the selling, in his early twenties, of a house in which he was born and raised by his grandparents until the age of eight. The house, the site of so many memories, conscious and unconscious, is the beginning of the story and, true to the mode of García Márquez, it is a beginning that precedes that of his life.

The shared memory of a community is the most evocative and passionate element in García Márquez's fiction, which is often narrated by an unidentified "we" who refer to the community that seems to understand itself as intuitively as an individual understands him- or herself. Often, the author seems to undercut—and thus examine—this most fundamental source of his voice by exploring the extremes of its opposite—solitude and amnesia, particularly through a significantly self-referential rhetoric of writing and inscription. García Márquez's representation of writing is convoluted and often highly ironic. It is the essential indication of solitude in many instances—most strongly in the cryptic parchment containing the fate of the Buendías in *One Hundred Years* and the feverish love letters of the young Fermina Daza and Florentino Ariza in *Love in the Time of Cholera*, both cases where writing and the deciphering of writing occur as a substitute for life and the experience of real community. However, in other instances, writing is the only defense against solitude and social decay, as in the time of Macondo's insomnia plague and the later letters of the aged Fermina Daza and Florentino Ariza.

In *One Hundred Years*, war and insomnia have the same effect of memory loss (as love and cholera evoke the same symptoms in *Love in the Time of Cholera*). Aureliano finally conceives of the idea to identify all objects with written labels so that no one will forget what each thing was called. His father José Arcadio Buendía extends this practice to the rest of the town, helping Macondo to preserve the genius of memory in written cues. José Arcadio Buendía affixes to each object its name and usual function so that the cow reads: *"This is the cow. She must be milked every morning so that she will produce milk, and the milked must be boiled in order to be mixed with coffee to make coffee and milk."*

The practice of writing is an odd function in Macondo and much of the fictional world of García Márquez, in which his characters employ writing in a manner that seems strictly functional, yet also strictly idiosyncratic in function to the writer and reader of the text. Roberto González Echevarría, in his essay, "Cien años de soledad: *The Novel as Myth and Archive*" presents a useful hypothesis regarding the function of the novel in the Latin American narrative. He writes: "It is my hypothesis that the novel, having no fixed form of its own, assumes that of a given document endowed with truth-bearing power by society at specific moments in history." The truth-bearing power of a document is the crux of the argument that inspires all the writing committed in the written world of García Márquez. José Arcadio Buendía's cow bears the sign proclaiming her significance in the strictly Buendían context of the morning milking ritual and coffee-drinking. In *The Autumn of the*

Patriarch, the ancient general writes desperate notes to himself to remember himself in his increasing senility. In *Love in the Time of Cholera*, when Florentino Ariza is thwarted in his love for Fermina Daza, he cannot quell his compulsion to write letters to his beloved. He resigns himself to writing letters on behalf of other lovers who commission his art on the street. Of course the ultimate notion of writing in the oeuvre of García Márquez is the parchment given to the Buendías by the gypsy Melquíades, which generations of solitary Buendías attempt unsuccessfully to decipher until the last of the line, the illegitimate and incestuous Aureliano. The meaning of the parchment forces the dark realization that he is reading his own demise, which has been scripted from the beginning of his line to the progressive present. The written truth of Melquíades and that of García Márquez, then, are seen to coincide in time and in meaning in the mind of the reader, who must read the act of reading of the last Aureliano in the final pages of *One Hundred Years* in order to realize the end of this breed of solitude. The bastard Aureliano reads in order to discover his origin as well as his end, even as his monstrous child, the Buendía born at last with the physical symbol of incest deferred over seven generations of close breeding is carried away by the red ants that have been devouring Úrsula's mansion from the time of the first Aureliano.

Love in the Time of Cholera also employs the motif of writing to resolve the tangles of fate. Florentino Ariza, the old composer of naïve passion, learns to refine his art for these new times, typing out letters to be mailed in business envelopes via the newly inaugurated mail service. Over seventy years old and having loved without reciprocation the one woman for fifty years, Florentino Ariza commences a mission of true self-representation in his one-sided correspondence to the beloved. After fifty years of estrangement, Florentino Ariza's letter reveals to Fermina Daza a man beyond her imagination who elucidates sentiments "just as she would have liked to say them," like a man "inspired by the Holy Spirit." The impression of spiritual inspiration is another motif that culminates in moments of climactic clarity for García Márquez's characters for whom matters of the spirit are often as mundane as the weather or dreams forgotten upon waking.

In the early years of *One Hundred Years*, the younger José Arcadio experiences spiritual awakening upon entering a gypsy girl: he "felt himself lifted up into the air toward a state of seraphic inspiration, where his heart burst forth with an outpouring of tender obscenities that entered the girl through her ears and came out of her mouth translated into her language." Here, as it was with Fermina Daza, inspiration and language are not far apart, so that when José Arcadio leaves Macondo with the gypsies, he returns years later with every last inch of his body covered with tattoos; even his phallus is inscribed with words in several languages entwined in red and blue. The multiple languages carved into José Arcadio's phallus in the two colors of the warring parties of his nation and the obscenities flowing from the gypsy girl's mouth in translation during intercourse are loaded examples of García Márquez's conflation of the motifs of writing, translation and inspiration. The altered person of José Arcadio, who has lost all familial instincts in exchange for revelry and social offense, is never again acceptable to the Buendía household. When he rapes and marries his foster sister Rebeca, he is expelled from the house and dies without reconciliation with his clan.

Among the many memorable women in the Buendía family, Rebeca is one of the most outstanding. An orphan who comes to the Buendías with a bag containing the bones of her parents and no explanations, she prefers to eat dirt and the whitewash that she peels from the walls with her nails, speaks not Spanish but the native Indian understood only by the servants, and infects the entire town with the plague of insomnia. After the death of her brother-husband, she locks herself up in her house until she becomes a living mummy—one of García Márquez's starkest characterizations of solitude in decay. As she is not biologically related to her adopted family, Rebeca had proposed a rare opportunity for genetic novelty for the inbred Buendías. However, when her endlessly postponed marriage to the Italian Pietro Crespi is ultimately thwarted by the return of José Arcadio, it is clear that the pattern of the family's misfortune infects and ruins even its adopted members.

Interestingly, the absolute meaninglessness of foreign novelty is a theme that García Márquez sneaks into the most domestic and seemingly mundane occasions in his narrative. Pietro Crespi, the unsuccessful suitor of Rebeca and then her sister, Amaranta, whose perverse rejection of the Italian results in his suicide, is an extreme example of the motif that the author scatters in the collected bric-a-brac throughout his fictional houses. The general in *The Autumn of the*

Patriarch signifies his anxiety by bringing unusual gifts to his mother and the woman that has become his obsession, the beauty queen Manuela Sánchez. In the course of her privileged life, Fermina Daza fills her house with trinkets from all over the world. She knows she buys them only for their novelty because "they were beautiful, useful objects as long as they remained in their original environment, in the show windows of Rome, Paris, London, or in New York ... [they] were worth their price not in gold but in the fleeting moment when someone from her local world would see them for the first time. For that is why they had been bought: so that others could see them." Ironically it is the death of her husband that provides the impetus for change. Fermina Daza, who had never been able to dispose of any of the objects that took up all the space in the house that should have been left for people, finally destroys the expensive rubbish and realizes that she will not miss these relics of her past.

Love in the Time of Cholera resuscitates the ravages of age that destroy the generations of Buendías in *One Hundred Years* and defeats the general of *The Autumn of the Patriarch* with a gentleness determined to achieve the redemption that cannot be found in the earlier novels. Whereas writing always underscores decay and destruction in his earlier works, García Márquez insists upon the restorative power of writing in his love story, where writing at last triumphs over death by disarming the past of the power of nostalgia. Where Melquíades' parchment inscribes a past moving toward the inevitable future, Florentino Ariza's autumnal letters to Fermina Daza work to erase the past to reveal a new future where they may no longer be threatened by impossible memories. Only when the impatient lover attempts to remind Fermina Daza of their youthful courtship does she recoil: "Why do you insist on talking about what does not exist?"

The question of what does and does not exist of the past is one that haunts the pages of García Márquez. In the novella *No One Writes to the Colonel* (1961), a colonel of Colonel Aureliano Buendías wars waits fifteen years in vain for the government's recognition of his pension, for which even his lawyer has lost the necessary documents. The government goes through the farce of documenting claims that will never be recognized, just as the lawyer continues to encourage his client whose case he has abandoned. When the neglected colonel finally demands that his lawyer present him with his proof of claim in order that he may take up his case with another lawyer, the former throws up his hands, protesting the impossibility of the task: "But those documents have passed through thousands and thousands of hands, in thousands and thousands of offices, before they reached God knows which department in the War Ministry.... It'll take centuries." The burden of account passes from office to office from year to year until no one remembers the location of the document much less its claim. The forgotten colonel, rather than accept the condition of his political and bureaucratic effacement, determines to continue his vigilance for his pension even as he and his aged wife literally starve. When she asks him in desperation what they are to eat in "the meantime" that they know will never end, he answers unforgettably: "Shit."

In another instance—one of the most pivotal events in García Márquez's fiction-from-reality—three thousand peacefully striking banana workers in the final generations of *One Hundred Years* are shot and killed by the army, then loaded up in two-hundred boxcars and dumped into the sea. José Arcadio Segundo, the sole survivor of the massacre, returns to Macondo to realize that everyone has accepted the government's statement that no one was harmed in the strike. He locks himself up in the room with seventy-two chambers pots and Melquíades' parchments reiterating the memory of the three thousand dead until he becomes literally invisible to the official eye and ostracized by his community who does not believe his "version" of the event. (In fact, after the ambiguously recorded event of the suppressed strike against United Fruit banana workers figured so prominently in *One Hundred Years*, public imagination largely assumed the historical accuracy of the casualty figure of three thousand despite the author's admission that the chosen number, which varies in official information, was his own notation. García Márquez's fictional account of reality came to be honored, in some cases, as reality itself—thereby performing one more instance of literally writing fate.) Like the colonel who discovers that the only right answer to the question that has been forgotten by the world but that has plagued him and his wife for fifteen years is the obscenity of excrement, José Arcadio Segundo becomes so consumed with the knowledge of an atrocity that no one will admit that he takes refuge in a room literally full of his own filth rather than deny what he cannot forget.

Solitude as the inevitable end for an unknown trauma is the

keystone that locks the characters of García Márquez into the vortex of memory and loss. In *The Autumn of the Patriarch*, García Márquez imagines the extreme of human solitude in the character of an unnamed military dictator, whose drive for absolute power over his country is a radical abstraction of the trauma that figures more literally as the fear of death or incest in his earlier works. The totalitarian regime of the general of *The Autumn* narrated by a seemingly indefatigable voice that seems to come from all angles to, from, and at the general, who is so isolated in his power that at his death no one can be sure of his identity because no one can confirm with certainty the features of his face as his.

In a close analysis of the symbol of the patriarch in *The Autumn*, Patricia Tobin, in her essay *"The Autumn of the Signifier: The Deconstructionist Moment of García Márquez,"* describes the novel as "a book for the head, a book that allows us to think the thoughts of our times," differentiating it from *One Hundred Years*, of which she writes: "It was the last moment of pure glee we were to enjoy before literary theory turned unholy and *unheimlich* on us." Her essay, which examines the character of the general from a rigorously post-structuralist point of view, invites an order—albeit negative—to this postmodern wasteland that disheartened devotees of the giddy magic realism of the Buendías' primeval Macondo.

García Márquez's patriarch—omnipotent but effectively invisible to the public, the object of confounded awe and terror—is in fact the farce of significance that attests to the deconstructionist identification of the absent center. The most significant event of the tyrant's life and the novel is the death of his official impostor, Patricio Aragonés. For three days, the general allows this death to be considered his own to discover the disloyalty of his closest attendants; he resurrects himself to oversee the summary execution of his false government. Thereafter, the narrator wisely learns: "We knew that no evidence of his death was final, because there was always another truth behind the truth." The real truth of the general's regime is more outrageous and more unfathomable than even the illusion of his power. The head of state resides in a veritable barnyard of beasts and runts, where the cows whose milk he supervises personally every morning mingle with his innumerable concubines and unrecognized offspring whose slim claim to legitimacy is the fact of premature birth that marks all the general's progeny. The general whose bureaucracy is a formality handles all matters of state as if each were an incident of personal errand, so that even his people have internalized without judgment the knowledge that the general must be absolved of all responsibility for all failures. When he hires the assassin José Ignacio Saenz de la Barra to avenge the deaths of his wife and son, and when that murderer systematically terrorizes the country, killing off scores of people and "martyrizing children under the age of five with electric wires on their testicles in order to force their parents to confess," the general is told:

> but you can sleep peacefully general sir, because the good patriots of the nation say that you know nothing, that all of this is going on without your consent, that if general sir knew it he would have sent Saenz de la Barra to push up daisies in the renegades' cemetery at the harbor fort, because every time they learned of a new act of barbarism they would sigh inside if the general only knew, if we could only make him know, if there were some way to see him and he ordered the one who had told him never to forget that the truth is I don't know anything, I haven't seen anything, I haven't talked about these things with anyone, and in that way he regained his calm, but so many sacks of severed heads kept arriving that it seemed inconceivable to him that José Ignacio Saenz de la Barra was daubing himself with blood up to his tonsure without some benefit from it … nor did it seem reasonable to him that whole years could pass without the commanders of the three services protesting over their subordinate status … he wanted to find out why they weren't trying to rebel, why they accepted the authority of a civilian …

The sentences that go on for hundreds of lines at a time, the chapters that are written as one long paragraph exhausts all perspectives in this novel, wherein one endless breath we hear 1) the narrator's account of 2) the general's attendant flattering the conscience of his leader by reiterating 3) the voice of the masses, which 4) returns the general to his own consciousness and paranoia regarding his suspended knowledge of all the above. The literary structure and tone of *The Autumn* makes violent shifts from pronoun to pronoun so that in this case, "you" addresses the general, as does "he," then "I" and finally the *narrative* "he," which comes from the subjective point of view of the general, distinct from the previous use of the same pronoun, which refers to him objectively in the course of public discourse.

Perhaps the most disorienting turn of perspective is that of the general regarding his mother, who often occurs in the narrative as "his mother of my life." Surpassing even the general in impenetrability, Bendición Alvarado is an inconceivable character whose paranoia at her son's deposal rouses avid instructions to "bury in a safe place the money you have left over from the government" because "you're only a general, so you're not good for anything except to command." As her son's power continues seemingly without end, however, Bendición Alvarado publicly begs God to send someone to overthrow her son despite his devotion to her throughout his rule, finally proclaiming her the Mother of the nation after his attempt to canonize her is rejected by the church.

In truth, Bendición Alvarado is a woman of no station that conceived her son in a moment of anonymous intercourse so that the patriarch of the nation, befitting García Márquez's classic characterization of solitude, is a bastard child that will never realize his origin or full identity. Neither is the search for (quasi-)divinity spared this most singular of men. Following the Buendían obsession of naming and (mis)interpretation, the general, failing to canonize his mother, names his one legitimate child Emanuel, "which is the name by which other gods know God." However, even this child is conceived out of wedlock and therefore unknown to the law of the God for whom he is named.

The compulsion to suffocate the natural progress of life with bogus interpretations that fill up a lifetime like the useless foreign objects that collect in the houses of García Márquez's imagination is given such free and powerful rein in the milieu of the patriarch that, unlike the fantastic explanations of the Buendía fathers, which only confuse and startle the Buendía children and in extreme cases, certain unnamed neighbors, an entire nation is held captivated by the worldview issued by the general's tyranny. Whereas the world is malleable because of the lack of proper names in Macondo, it is so in the autumn of the patriarch because there is nothing of true significance under the sun since truth could always be buried and resurrected and killed off again depending on the whims of an unknown man in a soldier's uniform without insignias. The general's regime exceeds the practice of interpretation of reality by imposing, above interpretation, official decrees of reality.

The moment of reversal and exposure that ultimately crumbles the illusion of absolute power reveals the deception that has sustained not only the fictional general in apparent inviolability but also the actual narrative, which has rendered to the reader in her reality the impression of power. The narrator first reveals, without ceremony or the notion of climax that the general keeps himself awake during the siesta hour so as to not lose the thread of his television movie, which

> since the times of José Ignacio Saenz de la Barra we had first installed an individual transmitter for the soap operas on the radio and then a closed-circuit television system so that only he would see the movies arranged to his taste in which no one died except the villains, love prevailed over death, life was a breath of fresh air, we made him happy with the trick as he had been so many afternoons of his old age with the girls in uniform who would have pleased him until his death if he had not had the bad luck to ask one of them what do they teach you in school and I told him the truth that they don't teach me anything sir, what I am is a waterfront whore, and he made her repeat it in case he hadn't understood well what he had read on my lips and I repeated it letter by letter that I'm not a student sir, I'm a waterfront whore, the sanitation service had bathed her in creolin and rinsed her off, they told her to put on this sailor suit and these nice-girl's stockings and go along this street every afternoon at five, not just me but all the whores of my age recruited and bathed by the sanitary police, all with the same uniform and the same men's shoes and these horsehair braid which look you can put on and take off like a comb …

The relatively innocuous admission of the closed-circuit television shows tailored to please the general's small imagination unfurls into a full exposé of the people's manipulation of his most intimate experience. Thus the reader, who is most likely unsympathetic to the character of the general, nevertheless experiences the absolute mortification of reality with him in this merciless anticlimax.

The first revelation, recounted by the communal "we" of the narrator, shifts to the "I" of the schoolgirl/whore, whose singularity voices the absolute complicity of the nation's fraud. The invisible community that evidently shares knowledge of the most sensitive state secrets seems at once near and far from the person of the general, who is close enough to hear the I of the confessing whore but is so outside her consciousness and the community it represents that she may announce her falsehood as matter-of-factly as one might explain the nature of one's homeland to a foreigner only superficially interested in the information. Thus the narrative structure of *The Autumn of the Patriarch* comes full circle. The dictator plays with the nature of truth and reality, believing in his omnipotence over the nation. For a century, that belief returns to him intact because his people submit to the charade. In the end the general is the game's solitary dunce, having lost both memory and sense, recognized by no one including himself.

As in the case of the impoverished colonel in *No One Writes to the Colonel*, whose impossible fate can only be expressed by obscenity, García Márquez often reaches the limits of signification to resolve—if that can be the right understanding of his narrative endings—the hopelessness of his characters. Indeed his is often a bleak vision that offers, to the solitary races of the earth, compassion and human forgiveness but not ultimately redemption, which is always suspended and hopefully deferred to an unnamed time. As is true for Fermina Daza and Florentino Ariza, who remain among the author's most hopeful characters as they quarantine their love in a falsified attack of cholera, the symptoms of solitary desire and nostalgia for the past may be disarmed forever but only by an impossible utopia of community and absolute intimacy.

GABRIEL GARCÍA MÁRQUEZ

The Solitude of Latin America

Antonio Pigafetta, a Florentine navigator who went with Magellan on the first voyage around the world, wrote, upon his passage through our southern lands of America, a strictly accurate account that nonetheless resembles a venture into fantasy. In it he recorded that he had seen hogs with navels on their haunches, clawless birds whose hens laid eggs on the backs of their mates, and others still, resembling tongueless pelicans, with beaks like spoons. He wrote of having seen a misbegotten creature with the head and ears of a mule, a camel's body, the legs of a deer and the whinny of a horse. He described how the first native encountered in Patagonia was confronted with a mirror, whereupon that impassioned giant lost his senses to the terror of his own image.

This short and fascinating book, which even then contained the seeds of our present-day novels, is by no means the most staggering account of our reality in that age. The Chronicles of the Indies left us countless others. Eldorado, our so avidly sought and illusory land, appeared on numerous maps for many a long year, shifting its place and form to suit the fantasy of cartographers. In his search for the fountain of eternal youth, the mythical Alvar Núñez Cabeza de Vaca explored the north of Mexico for eight years, in a deluded expedition whose members devoured each other and only five of whom returned, of the six hundred who had undertaken it. One of the many unfathomed mysteries of that

From *Nobel Lectures, Literature 1981–1990*, Editor-in-Charge Tore Frängsmyr, Editor Sture Allén, World Scientific Publishing Co., Singapore, 1993.

age is that of the eleven thousand mules, each loaded with one hundred pounds of gold, that left Cuzco one day to pay the ransom of Atahualpa and never reached their destination. Subsequently, in colonial times, hens were sold in Cartagena de Indias, that had been raised on alluvial land and whose gizzards contained tiny lumps of gold. One founder's lust for gold beset us until recently. As late as the last century, a German mission appointed to study the construction of an interoceanic railroad across the Isthmus of Panama concluded that the project was feasible on one condition: that the rails not be made of iron, which was scarce in the region, but of gold.

Our independence from Spanish domination did not put us beyond the reach of madness. General Antonio López de Santana, three times dictator of Mexico, held a magnificent funeral for the right leg he had lost in the so-called Pastry War. General Gabriel García Moreno ruled Ecuador for sixteen years as an absolute monarch; at his wake, the corpse was seated on the presidential chair, decked out in full-dress uniform and a protective layer of medals. General Maximiliano Hernández Martínez, the theosophical despot of El Salvador who had thirty thousand peasants slaughtered in a savage massacre, invented a pendulum to detect poison in his food, and had streetlamps draped in red paper to defeat an epidemic of scarlet fever. The statue to General Francisco Morazán erected in the main square of Tegucigalpa is actually one of Marshal Ney, purchased at a Paris warehouse of second-hand sculptures.

Eleven years ago, the Chilean Pablo Neruda, one of the outstanding poets of our time, enlightened this audience with his word. Since then, the Europeans of good will—and sometimes those of bad, as well—have been struck, with ever greater force, by the unearthly tidings of Latin America, that boundless realm of haunted men and historic women, whose unending obstinacy blurs into legend. We have not had a moment's rest. A promethean president, entrenched in his burning palace, died fighting an entire army, alone; and two suspicious airplane accidents, yet to be explained, cut short the life of another great-hearted president and that of a democratic soldier who had revived the dignity of his people. There have been five wars and seventeen military coups; there emerged a diabolic dictator who is carrying out, in God's name, the first Latin American ethnocide of our time. In the meantime, twenty million Latin American children died before the age of one—more than have been born in Europe since 1970. Those missing because of repression number nearly one hundred and twenty thousand, which is as if no one could account for all the inhabitants of Uppsala. Numerous women arrested while pregnant have given birth in Argentine prisons, yet nobody knows the whereabouts and identity of their children who were furtively adopted or sent to an orphanage by order of the military authorities. Because they tried to change this state of things, nearly two hundred thousand men and women have died throughout the continent, and over one hundred thousand have lost their lives in three small and ill-fated countries of Central America: Nicaragua, El Salvador and Guatemala. If this had happened in the United States, the corresponding figure would be that of one million six hundred thousand violent deaths in four years.

One million people have fled Chile, a country with a tradition of hospitality—that is, ten per cent of its population. Uruguay, a tiny nation of two and a half million inhabitants which considered itself the continent's most civilized country, has lost to exile one out of every five citizens. Since 1979, the civil war in El Salvador has produced almost one refugee every twenty minutes. The country that could be formed of all the exiles and forced emigrants of Latin America would have a population larger than that of Norway.

I dare to think that it is this outsized reality, and not just its literary expression, that has deserved the attention of the Swedish Academy of Letters. A reality not of paper, but one that lives within us and determines each instant of our countless daily deaths, and that nourishes a source of insatiable creativity, full of sorrow and beauty, of which this roving and nostalgic Colombian is but one cipher more, singled out by fortune. Poets and beggars, musicians and prophets, warriors and scoundrels, all creatures of that unbridled reality, we have had to ask but little of imagination, for our crucial problem has been a lack of conventional means to render our lives believable. This, my friends, is the crux of our solitude.

And if these difficulties, whose essence we share, hinder us, it is understandable that the rational talents on this side of the world, exalted in the contemplation of their own cultures, should have found themselves without valid means to interpret us. It is only natural that they insist on measuring us with the yardstick that they use for themselves, forgetting that the ravages of life are not the same for all, and that the quest of our own identity is just as arduous and bloody for us as it was for them. The interpretation of our reality through patterns not our own, serves only to make us ever more unknown, ever less free, ever more solitary. Venerable Europe would perhaps be more perceptive if it tried to see us in its own past. If only it recalled that London took three hundred years to build its first city wall, and three hundred years more to acquire a bishop; that Rome labored in a gloom of uncertainty for twenty centuries, until an Etruscan King anchored it in history; and that the peaceful Swiss of today, who feast us with their mild cheeses and apathetic watches, bloodied Europe as soldiers of fortune, as late as the Sixteenth Century. Even at the height of the Renaissance, twelve thousand lansquenets in the pay of the imperial armies sacked and devastated Rome and put eight thousand of its inhabitants to the sword.

I do not mean to embody the illusions of Tonio Kröger, whose dreams of uniting a chaste north to a passionate south were exalted here, fifty-three years ago, by Thomas Mann. But I do believe that those clear-sighted Europeans who struggle, here as well, for a more just and humane homeland, could help us far better if they reconsidered their way of seeing us. Solidarity with our dreams will not make us feel less alone, as long as it is not translated into concrete acts of legitimate support for all the peoples that assume the illusion of having a life of their own in the distribution of the world.

Latin America neither wants, nor has any reason, to be a pawn without a will of its own; nor is it merely wishful thinking that its quest for independence and originality should become a Western aspiration. However, the navigational advances that have narrowed such distances between our Americas and Europe seem, conversely, to have accentuated our cultural remoteness. Why is the originality so readily granted us in literature so mistrustfully denied us in our difficult attempts at social change? Why think that the social justice sought by progressive Europeans for their own countries cannot also be a goal for Latin America, with different methods for dissimilar conditions? No: the immeasurable violence and pain of our history are the result of age-old inequities and untold bitterness, and not a conspiracy plotted three thousand leagues from our home. But many European leaders and thinkers have thought so, with the childishness of old-timers who have forgotten the fruitful excess of their youth as if it were impossible to find another destiny than to live at the mercy of the two great masters of the world. This, my friends, is the very scale of our solitude.

In spite of this, to oppression, plundering and abandonment, we respond with life. Neither floods nor plagues, famines nor cataclysms, nor even the eternal wars of century upon century, have been able to subdue the persistent advantage of life over death. An advantage that grows and quickens: every year, there are seventy-four million more births than deaths, a sufficient number of new lives to multiply, each year, the population of New York sevenfold. Most of these births occur in the countries of least resources—including, of course, those of Latin America. Conversely, the most prosperous countries have succeeded in accumulating powers of destruction such as to annihilate, a hundred times over, not only all the human beings that have existed to this day, but also the totality of all living beings that have ever drawn breath on this planet of misfortune.

On a day like today, my master William Faulkner said, "I decline to accept the end of man". I would fall unworthy of standing in this place that was his, if I were not fully aware that the colossal tragedy he refused to recognize thirty-two years ago is now, for the first time since the beginning of humanity, nothing more than a simple scientific possibility. Faced with this awesome reality that must have seemed a mere utopia through all of human time, we, the inventors of tales, who will believe anything, feel entitled to believe that it is not yet too late to engage in the creation of the opposite utopia. A new and sweeping utopia of life, where no one will be able to decide for others how they die, where love will prove true and happiness be possible, and where the races condemned to one hundred years of solitude will have, at last and forever, a second opportunity on earth.

GERALD MARTIN

On 'Magical' and Social Realism
in García Márquez

Although you have every right not to believe me after
putting up for so long with my sly tricks and
falsifications, I swear to you by the bones of my mother
that what I am now about to show you is no illusion but
the plain and simple truth ...
(García Márquez, 'Blacamán the Good, miracle-salesman')

What interested me in my novel was above all to tell
the story of a family obsessed by incest, and which; in
spite of every precaution taken for several generations,
ends up having a child with a strange pig's tail.
(García Márquez on *One Hundred Years of Solitude*, 1968)

The true history of Latin America is as yet an almost
totally blank book, save for a few phrases recorded in
such equivocal terms that no one troubles to try and
understand them ... Through misinterpreting their
past, Latin Americans construct false projects for the
future, and every step they take in the present in
accordance with those projects, vitiated by that initial
falseness, only serves to sink them deeper in their

From *Gabriel García Márquez: New Readings*, Bernard McGuirk and Richard Cardwell, ed.
© Cambridge University Press, 1987.

sickness, as in a circle from which there is no way out.
(H.A. Murena, *The Original Sin of America*)

> They wanted nothing to do with that series of conflicts,
> revolts, alternations between dictatorship and anarchy.
> In past history they found nothing constructive,
> nothing they aspired to be. And yet, in spite of
> everything, the Latin American was making history,
> not the history he would have wished for, but his own
> history. A very special history, with no negations or
> dialectical assimilations. A history full of contradictions
> that never came to synthesis. But history for all that.
> The history that we Latin Americans, half-way through
> the twentieth century, must negate dialectically, that is,
> assimilate.

(Leopoldo Zea, *The Latin American Mind*)

> Beyond this general collapse of Reason and Faith, God
> and Utopia, there are no intellectual systems old or
> new to be erected, capable of appeasing our anguish or
> relieving our dismay: there is nothing before us. We are
> finally alone. Like all men ... Out there, in the open
> solitude, transcendence also awaits us: the hands of
> other solitary beings. We are, for the first time in our
> history, the contemporaries of all men.

(Octavio Paz, *The Labyrinth of Solitude*)

A few long weeks ago, already in the iron grip of disenchantment
and waves of *déjà vu* (this is written from Portsmouth a year after the war
in the South Atlantic which has rekindled the dying embers of so many
national myths), I chanced again on some earlier meditations on distant
'South America' recorded by Lord Byron in 1809: 'Europe's
decrepitude', he lamented, 'is increasing; everybody here is the same,
everything repeats itself. There the people are as fresh as their New
World, and as violent as their earthquakes.'[1] We Europeans, one reflects,
have always viewed Latin America, like Africa, through all the twists and
turns of a long historical relationship (it will soon be 1992), as alternately
the earthly paradise or the heart of darkness, their inhabitants as noble

or ignoble savages, according to the opportune requirements of the moment. Although awareness of the stratagems involved has increased markedly since the appearance of works by Fanon, Memmi, Césaire and Fernández Retamar (*Caliban*), and especially now that Said has studied 'Orientalism' and Todorov the conquest of America from the standpoint of 'Otherness', a majority of readers of fiction in this country remain curiously and conveniently innocent of them. But it is only such ideological self-awareness which, in my opinion, can provide the framework essential for any serious investigation into the deceptively transparent writing of Colombia's Gabriel García Márquez.

The 1982 Nobel Prize winner has repeatedly declared that nothing of importance happened to him after the death of his beloved grandfather, the Colonel, when he was eight years old, so that his novels are suffused with the emotions and memories of those early years, and therefore, one might add, by a nostalgic quest—many years later—for that lost time. It was at a similar age that I, almost a century and a half after Byron, infant inhabitant of a grey post-war London, first began, on the basis of two or three postage stamps of volcanoes and cactuses, the *Wonder Book of the Amazon Jungle*, and the Hollywood trail down Mexico way, to invent a world for myself, the multicoloured new world of Latin America. My nostalgia was for a reality I had never known, and what I invented was something rather like the exotic literary phenomenon critics now call 'magical realism'. Needless to say, I knew nothing of the fabulous imaginings of the Spanish *conquistadores*, the innocent primitive engendered by the Enlightenment, or the *Volksgeist* conceived by the Romantics; nor of the metamorphoses involved as such concepts lived on into the Surrealist 1920s. Indeed, I was a distinctly reluctant, if bemused witness to the age of decolonization, shortly before the next— now 'Third World'—nativist tide began to flow in the 1960s, with its grotesque reflections in Western hippiedom and psychedelia. Yet, when I began to study Latin America at university in those early sixties, it seemed that all I had invented was really true: here indeed was a comic opera world of fantasy and magic, generals and doctors, beggars on golden stools. I recall the impact upon me of one of the first texts I read, Sarmiento's archetypal *Facundo: Civilization and Barbarism*, in which I learned—and I wanted to believe it—that in 1833, in a province of 400,000 inhabitants, only three had voted against the tyrant Rosas; or that the same Rosas's mother had insisted, to the end of her days, on the family servants ministering to her on their knees (part III, 2). I did not suspect that magic had turned to reality for Rosas, that he had ceased to be colourful when, at the end of his life long ago, he came to die in faraway Hampshire.

In 1965, the year in which Parry reported on the lost Seaborne Empire, I bought the now famous Latin America number of *Encounter* (funded by the CIA), and, in a hallucinatory article on *la violencia* by Malcolm Deas,[2] was persuaded that Colombians were every bit as bizarre and hyperbolic in reality as García Márquez, two years later, would show them to be in his fictional *One Hundred Years of Solitude*. Like Latin Americans themselves, though without the same bitter contradictions, we roar with laughter at the ridiculous egocentricity of these fictional characters, these South Americans: but our own ethnocentricity is no laughing matter. Later that year I too finally travelled to Latin America, as I had done so often in my imagination; and slowly, incredulously, began to realize that I did not, after all, believe in fairies, and that even fantasy and magic have their own histories, their own secret motivation.

One Hundred Years of Solitude, despite the occasional carelessness and repetitiveness of some of its writing, can justly lay claim to being, perhaps, the greatest of all Latin American novels, appropriately enough, since the story of the Buendía family is obviously a metaphor for the history of the continent since Independence, that is, for the neocolonial period. More than that, though, it is also, I believe, a narrative about the *myths* of Latin American history. If this is where its true importance lies, it is also the reason why so many readers have become lost in its shimmering hall of mirrors. And if each reader inevitably interprets the novel according to his or her own ideological preconceptions, one must be skeptical of some of the unconscious motives behind its astonishing success in the still imperialistic English-speaking world, where, after all, very few Latin American novels have gone before.

It is instructive in this, as in other ways, to compare and contrast García Márquez with Borges. However 'Argentine' Borges may or may not be (and one would not wish to reopen this largely tautological debate), he went into production, to put it crudely, with a top-quality luxury product aimed implicitly at the European consumer. It proved a highly marketable finished commodity, albeit a minority one. García

Márquez's work shows every sign of having been manufactured for the home market, Latin America, and yet it has been just as acceptable to European and North American—which is to say, 'universal'—taste. He became the first truly international best-seller in Latin American publishing history.[3] If, as I believe, part of the novel's achievement is a socialist—though not a 'social realist'—reading of Latin American history, the most likely explanation for its sensational success in, say, Britain and the United States is that its subtle ambiguities make it as possible for readers to despise or sympathize with its Latin American characters as it would be in life outside the novel. None of this is so surprising. Almost four hundred years after Cervantes wrote *Don Quixote*, critics continue to assure us that it is about some eternal or frozen distinction between reality and illusion, rather than—as seems evident to me—about a nostalgia (deeply felt by its author but all the more strongly satirized for that in its characters) for a mythologized aristocratic world-view in an age of mercantilist relations. *One Hundred Years of Solitude*, it is arguable, was born of a nostalgic longing for certain pre-capitalist rural relations in an age of rapid urbanization and the implantation of industrial capitalism. Perhaps the most 'limpid' and transparent works are, in reality, the most opaque.

This is why, although it is tempting to write in an abstract and sophisticated manner about the works of García Márquez, it is not the approach that I intend to take. Certainly he is a master of magic and mystery, and his writing is so consistently *enjoyable* that one frequently forgets that to believe, even temporarily, in illusions is to settle for a world that is undecipherable and unknowable. But this is surely not the job of criticism. My view is that the essential point of departure for any comprehensive analysis of *One Hundred Years of Solitude* must be an examination of its perception of the relation between ideology and consciousness, and between lived reality, historiography and literature. More precisely, whilst a number of the novel's central themes and achievements are not in doubt (though we shall be forced to reiterate them), I believe that García Márquez criticism as a whole has suffered from three basic errors, particularly with reference to studies of *One Hundred Years of Solitude*:

(1) Critics have failed to perceive that history is not only devoured by myth, as is so frequently claimed,[4]

but that every myth also has its history. This novel is
not about 'history-and-myth', but about the myths of
history and their demystification.

(2) They fail to differentiate correctly between the
perspective of the novelist and that of his characters, an
elementary distinction with infinitely complex
ramifications in this most subtle yet apparently
straightforward text.

(3) They largely ignore the context, historical and
literary, in which the novel was written and published.

An approach based on these three perceptions can guide us to a
more satisfactory reading of the novel, in particular to a convincing
interpretation of its ending, and can explain to us García Márquez's
standpoint on 'time' and 'magic', history and society. It can also help to
demystify critical terminology itself and perhaps dispel the optical
illusions of such pernicious—even racist—ideologies as those which
underpin the concept of 'magical realism'.

Donald Shaw, in an invaluable review of responses to *One Hundred
Years of Solitude*, indicates what for him is its basic critical problem: 'the
fact that the novel appears to function on three different levels of
meaning: one related to the nature of reality, a second concerned with
universal human destiny and a third connected with the problems of
Latin America'.[5] He later argues: 'What is important, however, is that
such pathways towards the understanding of the novel should not be
followed separately, as has mainly been the case hitherto, but explored
simultaneously with the fullest recognition of their implications for one
another.'[6] I agree with Shaw that the three dimensions (ontological,
epistemological, historical) are each of comparable importance in this as
in all great works of artistic fiction. Where I would differ is in my belief
that García Márquez's apparent underlying tragic vision is not *necessarily*
in contradiction with a revolutionary standpoint on Latin American
development. Indeed, the view that I would propose is that in *One
Hundred Years of Solitude*, García Márquez momentarily found a means of
reconciling his rather evident philosophical pessimism (of a 'Leopardian'
materialist variety, to echo Timpanaro) with his determinedly optimistic
conception of the march of history. It is perhaps through this tension
that the novel has attained its undeniable classic status.[7] Clearly, though,

as Shaw argues, everything ultimately rests on one's interpretation of the apocalyptic conclusion, and I shall return to this problem below.

Although the topic under discussion here—how magical and how realist is García Márquez?—is relevant to all his fictional production (not excluding some of his journalism),[8] *One Hundred Years of Solitude* (1967) remains the pivotal work, and by far the most complex. In *Leafstorm* (1955), *In Evil Hour* (1962), or, quintessentially, *No One Writes to the Colonel* (1958), the basic narrative conventions are those of critical realism, with implicit but perfectly straightforward economic, social and political (that is, historical) explanations for the psychological motivations of each of the characters (Angel Rama speaks of 'a pronounced social determinism').[9] Any picturesqueness in them is no more than eccentricity born of ex-centricity. In the much later *The Autumn of the Patriarch* (1975), on the other hand, the weakness for hyperbole—what J. Mejía Duque has called 'the crisis of disproportion'[10]—and the temptation of the *tour de force* between them sweep almost all grasp on historical reality away, and it is worth recalling that the novel was written in Spain, where García Márquez was living during the last seven years of the Franco regime. In this novel he appears—doubtless it is the price of playing to the gallery—to become lost in the same ideological and linguistic labyrinths into which he had unintentionally lured so many other unsuspecting writers with the glittering success of *One Hundred Years of Solitude*. That work, it seems to me, remains the only text of his in which the mix of real and fantasy elements is both perfectly fused and, analytically—as I interpret it— perfectly separable.[11]

Dualisms, even manichaeisms, of every kind, while entirely explicable in terms of Latin America's colonial experience, are frequently the bane of its literature and criticism. Angel Rama, in his early article on García Márquez, noted 'an oscillation in the author himself with regard to the plane on which any given explanation should rest: whether on the social or the metaphysical level'.[12] By the time of *One Hundred Years of Solitude*, however, the technical sleight of hand had become almost invisible, and most critics began to emphasize the blend of myth and history, fiction and reality, and to view with approval the apparent impossibility of distinguishing between them. Julio Ortega insisted that 'the play of reality and fantasy is never dual in this novel';[13] José Miguel Oviedo declared that the novelist had 'mixed the real and the fantastic in so perfect and inextricable a fashion that no one can tell where the frontier between them may lie';[14] and Ernst Völkening commented admiringly that García Márquez was blessed with 'the uncommon gift of seeing both sides of the moon at one and the same time'.[15]

This, then, is the novel which, perhaps more than any other, has been taken to confirm the historical demise of social realism in Latin American fiction and to herald the arrival of the linguistic, experimental or post-Modernist novel. Such social realism, as most critics now agree, dominated the period from about 1915, the moment of Mariano Azuela's *Los de abajo* (*The Underdogs*) and other novels of the Mexican Revolution, to about 1945, when writers like Asturias, Borges and Carpentier came into view. But to see things this way seems to me an over-simplification of Latin American literary history and a misreading of *One Hundred Years of Solitude* itself, which contains a greater variety of carefully encoded material relating to the positivistic orders of social psychology, political economy and the history of ideas than almost any other Latin American novel that comes to mind. Angel Rama's verdict on García Márquez's early works, already disconcerting to most readers, seems to me to be equally applicable to *One Hundred Years of Solitude* itself: 'I do not believe any other novelist has so acutely, so truthfully seen the intimate relationship between the socio-political structure of a given country and the behaviour of his characters.'[16] The main reason why so many readers have missed these otherwise obvious facts is that García Márquez presents most aspects of reality from the standpoint of his characters, while he himself, as narrator, adopts a perspective based—largely but not entirely ironically, in which lies much of the difficulty—on the mainly metaphysical views of the *pensadores* ('thinkers'), those ideologists who dominated Latin America's interpretation of its own history until after the Second World War. Sarmiento's struggle between civilization and barbarism, Rodó's exaltation of Ariel against Caliban; the sick continent diagnosed by Bunge and Arguedas, Keyserling's swamp-like dawn of creation and *tristeza criolla* (creole sadness), Martínez Estrada's view of Latin Americans as victims of a historical mirage, Mallea's incommunicability, and—above all—Murena's original sin thesis:[17] these and many other weird and wonderful theories of American history jostle for supremacy throughout the novel, only to find themselves circumscribed, at the last, by a conception which coincides closely with the rather more lucid kinds of perspective that emerged in Mexico after 1945, namely Paz's assertion that Latin Americans were now the contemporaries of all men and Zea's thesis that it was time, at long last, to break out of the labyrinth of solitude and assimilate the history of the continent. Seen like this, there is perhaps more to García Márquez's work than the echoes of Faulkner, Borges and other such literary influences so widely debated by some critics.

If this conception of *One Hundred Years of Solitude* is accepted, all the hallowed references to Vico, Hegel and Croce, all talk of circularities and eternal returns become redundant. It is for this reason that for me the most convincing interpretations of the novel's apparent dualism have come from critics with a sociological approach, above all Agustín Cueva, who argues that García Márquez 'is not seeking to put forward an irrationalist philosophy but merely to recreate a representation of a world that he knows is over and done with'.[18] Cueva shows that the work is a synthesis of elements belonging to two different genres, the epic and the novel, a line later followed by Todorov, who likewise brings out the clash between an individualist and a collective view of the world.[19] Similarly, Sergio Benvenuto, in a brilliant short study, affirms that 'living contradiction is the only appropriate language for this incredible intersection of universal culture and local unculture'.[20]

To those who know Latin America, the culture traits in the text are unmistakable, though each is almost impossible to extricate from its anecdotic materiality; to those who do not know the continent, the novel is more abstract, and the incidents are recognizable as vehicles of universal experiences or truths distorted by Latin American eccentricity. Thus almost everything is at once familiar but unidentifiable inside this literary 'aleph': we see the world from genesis to apocalypse, from Renaissance to Baroque, from independence to neocolonialism; or from use values to exchange values, transparence to opaqueness, childhood innocence to adult guilt, lines and circles to labyrinths. The result has been called magical realism. The problem is that the same term is used, consciously or unconsciously, as an ideological stratagem to collapse many different kinds of writing, and many different political perspectives, into one single, usually escapist, concept.[21] Like the Surrealist movement from which it ultimately derives, magical realism might in part be seen as an unconscious—irony of ironies!—conspiracy between European or North American critics eager to get away, in their imagination, to the colourful world of Latin America, and certain Latin American writers desperate to take refuge, in their writing, from the injustice and brutality of their continent's unacceptable reality. This makes detailed analysis of every case particularly important. There is a world of difference between the view that tacitly assumes that reality itself is or may be fantastic, or that the imagination is autonomous (Borges, Lezama Lima, sometimes Cortázar) and a perspective which takes seriously the religious beliefs or myths, the fantasies or illusions of the fictional characters, whether by reproducing them 'anthropologically' or by critically demystifying them (Asturias, Carpentier, Rulfo, Roa Bastos and—in this but not all cases—García Márquez). If the term must be used, it is best confined to the latter kind of writing, in which, essentially, there is a dialectic between pre-scientific and scientific visions of reality, seen most clearly in works which combine the mythological or folk beliefs of the characters with the consciousness of a twentieth-century observer. Although García Márquez is by no means always clear about the distinction in all his fiction, I believe that *One Hundred Years of Solitude* at least is entirely coherent in this regard and that it is to this in large measure that it owes the unparalleled breadth and depth of its critical and popular success. Our difficulty is that the two levels are really separable only on the abstract plane of analysis, so seriously does the omniscient narrator take the beliefs of his characters. García Márquez uses a battery of complementary literary techniques—above all, caricature, hyperbole, bathos and condensation of every kind—to unite the two levels in each and every anecdote of his narrative.

The fact remains that a majority of critics and general readers appear to admire the novel precisely because, in their view, it conjures up a magical reality. Let us therefore examine this. In order to demonstrate such a view—and herein lies the contradiction—one has to know what reality is. So herewith an elementary hypothesis: whatever contemporary reality may be, it is determined and defined by the metropolitan centres of culture in Europe and, above all now, the United States. As Marx and Engels noted, 'The ruling ideas of each age have ever been the ideas of its ruling class ...' Latin America can therefore be viewed, by definition, as a home of irreality, where people are larger or smaller than life: there for my entertainment, specimens in the national-geographical catalogue of planetary showbiz safaris (in short, less than human). Critics accordingly praise the novel for its further confirmation that life is a dream, whereas it is, to say the least, plausible that what the novel is saying is that *Latin American life* is a dream—the 'unreality' and 'unauthenticity' imposed by almost five hundred years of colonialism—and that when a dream becomes a permanent living nightmare it is probably time to wake up.[22] The official history which 'Europe' has projected is that of rationalism, capitalism, progressive development and linear chronology. However contradictory and repressive this history may seem to any European, it is, for the typical Latin American, organic and coherent: by definition; whereas his own history is fragmented, discontinuous, absurd ('time itself underwent jolts and accidents, and thus could splinter and leave an eternalized instant in a room').[23] It is his fate actually to be one of the despised inhabitants of a 'banana republic', victim of a 'comic-opera regime' or a 'tin-pot junta': He is a 'mimic man'. Or so 'we' would have him think.

In *One Hundred Years of Solitude* nothing ever turns out as people expect; everything surprises them; all of them fail; all are frustrated; few achieve communion with others for more than a fleeting moment, and the majority not at all. Most of their actions—at first sight like the structure of the novel as a whole—are circular (*hacer para deshacer*: 'doing in order to undo'). Ploughers of the sea, they are unable to make their lives purposive, achieve productiveness, break out of the vicious circle of their fate. In short, they fail to become agents of history for themselves: like the characters of Rulfo's *Pedro Páramo* (1955), they are the echoes of someone else's history, the last link in the centre–periphery chain.[24] The only explanation possible is that they are living out their lives in the name of someone else's values. Hence the solitude, central theme (together with the quest) of Latin American history: it is their abandonment in an empty continent, a vast cultural vacuum, marooned thousands of miles away from their true home. Conceived by Spain in the sixteenth century (the stranded galleon, the buried suit of armour), the characters awaken in the late eighteenth-century Enlightenment (magnet and telescope as symbols of the two pillars of Newtonian physics), but are entirely unable to bring themselves into focus in a world they have not made. Influences from outside (the gypsies) are sporadic, piecemeal, throughout the notional hundred years of the novel, which is the span from the Independence era to the early 1960s, when it was being written.

Of course the characters are supposed—by themselves, at least—to be living in 'our' world. Times of the day, days of the week, statistics of every kind are to be found everywhere in the novel, but are no more helpful or meaningful than the more obviously illusory temporal references such as 'many years later' which appear with equal frequency, from its very first sentence. The characters all believe that their actions are purposive, but whenever they follow their logical chain to its conclusion they find that they have come in a circle. Yet, despite the historical immobility which lies at its heart, the narrative literally teems with actions (part of its revival of the 'forgotten art of story-telling', to use Gullón's phrase).[25]

One Hundred Years of Solitude is the domain of the verb. The actions of which the verbs tell are individualistic, usually to the point of an extraordinary egotism—at least on the part of the male characters—and such individualism, given its relation to liberal ideology, might seem to suggest that they were genuinely historical, occurring only once in time and contributing more or less consciously to the movement of human history. But, once the reader is immersed in the narrative, each action begins to remind him of many other actions, since their inner meanings, like the names of the characters, constantly recur and refer, giving such apparently Borgesian concepts as the labyrinth and the mirror an inescapably material reading. Thus the very individualism and self-centredness of the characters is an obsessively repeated ritual. The fountain-head of this form of unreality is the first José Arcadio Buendía. It is he, progenitor of the novel, who, soon after the start, initiates the pattern of bemused *contemplation*, self-absorption and withdrawal. The Aurelianos, by contrast, are actively selfish and individualistic, seekers of power rather than knowledge. Ursula, who has been much studied, is the paradigm of the commonsensical mother figure, symbol of an entire epoch of family relations, but herself comes to believe that everything is circular (that the present is subordinate to the past), a conviction which brings her death and prompts the death of many others. Curiously enough, she makes her discovery, as we shall see, at precisely the moment when history, and the consciousness of modernity, has finally broken through to Macondo.

At this point, then, the Buendía line is doomed. I take this to mean that neocolonialism is at an end, remembering that the novel was written during the early years of the Cuban Revolution. There seems little doubt that the morbid fear of the birth of a child cursed with a pig's tail is a condensed metaphor for the combined ideologies of original sin and biological determinism (so that, again, esoteric or essentialist arguments about the nature and meaning of the incest theme seem to me beside the point, and appear to have given García Márquez almost endless amusement). The former circumscribed the whole of life in the colonial period, and was overlain by the latter after Independence, as an explanation of Latin America's continuing backwardness and a positivist justification of the rule of Europeanized minorities. (If we take the term *estirpe*—stock, lineage—literally, we have merely been lured into the same ideological misreading as the characters themselves: it is a historical era that is over, not a biological line). The impact of Darwin and Spencer produced the ideologies of Bunge and Arguedas in the early twentieth century, at a time when the European powers and the United States were still extending their colonial possessions. The reflection of these overlapping religious, philosophical and scientific theories in the self-image of the characters brings about an immensely subtle tragicomic fusion of fatalism and individualism. Most of the characters are aware that others have weaknesses and are doomed to failure, yet none of them know this about themselves. The secret last analysis of every situation reverts to racial or metaphysical explanations. If you call a child Aureliano, he will turn out like 'an Aureliano'. There is no escape; and no second chance. Problems of underdevelopment, dependency or imperialism never occur to these characters (they have occurred to the author, but, like Borges's Pierre Menard, his genius lies in having apparently managed to 'forget' them.) They are blissfully unaware of historical reality and know nothing of the world which has determined their destiny. Their only thoughts or memories are about things which relate to the structure of the novel; which is therefore the very fabric of their perceived social history. This explains the exoticism, for them, of phenomena which to us are quite normal—it is to our discredit if we can still find this surprising or amusing—as it also explains the often cited dreamlike quality of the Banana Company massacre narrated in the later part of the text.

Seen in this light, the novel seems less concerned with any 'magical' reality than with the general effect of a colonial history upon individual relationships: hence the themes of circularity, irrationality, fatalism, isolation, superstition, fanaticism, corruption and violence.

The judgement as to whether these traits are inherent or produced by history is as much a political as a philosophical or scientific determination.

Even among critics who would follow me this far in the argument, there is little agreement about the meaning of the conclusion. Whilst not wishing to over-simplify it, I believe that it, too, is more straightforward than most readers have imagined. An old-fashioned biographical approach, as followed by Vargas Llosa in his pathbreaking critical study, can give us the first clue.[26] A number of critics have recognized the strike against the Banana Company and the ensuing massacre as the central shaping episode of the entire novel, though few have realized just how much this is the case. It is the theme of proletarian struggle, however, which is the secret thread that can guide us out into the light at the end of the labyrinth. García Márquez was born in 1928, the very year in which the historic massacre took place. It is at about the same time that Meme Buendía's son, the illegitimate Aureliano, is born in the novel. His mother had been forbidden to see Mauricio, his father, because, as an apprentice mechanic in the company workshop and one-time employee of Aureliano Triste, he was from an inferior class. Mauricio's surname is Babilonia, conceivably because the proletariat, which he represents, will bring about the historical destruction of 'Macondo', which is less a place than the name García Márquez gives to an era. Interestingly, Mauricio looks like a gypsy (p. 242), which suggests that as a migrant manual worker, a member of the *hojarasca* ('trash') so despised by García Márquez's own family when he was a child, he is a vehicle of the same kind of internationalist consciousness and impact (what the Mexican government now calls 'exotic influences') as the real gypsies led by Melquiades in the earlier sections of the novel. Mauricio is permanently crippled in an accident at the end of chapter 14, shortly after Meme becomes pregnant, and appears no more. But, at the beginning of chapter 15, the arrival of his illegitimate son is made to coincide explicitly with the author's own prophesy of doom for Macondo: 'The events which were to deal Macondo its mortal blow were already on the horizon when they brought Meme Buendía's son home' (p. 249).

These apocalyptic 'events' are *historical* ones. It is of course Aureliano Babilonia himself who will eventually decipher Melquiades's parchments on the final page. All the disasters to come had in fact already been presaged by a previous textual moment, at the end of chapter 11, through a familiar image of progress: 'the innocent yellow train that was to bring so many insecurities and uncertainties, so many joys and misfortunes, so many changes, calamities and nostalgias to Macondo' (p. 193). The decision to bring the yellow train, inaugurating the final stage in the penetration of Macondo's introversion and self-centredness, was taken by Aureliano Triste, the man who turned the magical ice into a commodity, which we can construe as representative of the embryonic local bourgeoisie: 'they remembered him well because in a matter of hours he had managed to destroy every breakable object that passed through his hands' (p. 191). The train in its turn brings the multinational Banana Company, United States imperialism, and eventual disaster, a perfectly logical sequence of events carefully explained by the author himself, all of which has little to do with pigs' tails.

The Banana Company brings temporary prosperity around the time of the First World War, but as profits are threatened in the late 1920s the workers begin strike action. José Arcadio Segundo, great-uncle of the baby Aureliano Babilonia, and at first a foreman in the company, becomes a trade union leader and plays a leading role in the conflict. He is one of the few survivors of the massacre, and insists on repeating his eye-witness account of the death of more than three thousand demonstrators until the day he dies. Indeed, his last words—to none other than Aureliano Babilonia, in Melquíades's old but ageless room—are: 'Always remember that there were more than three thousand and that they threw them in the sea' (p. 300). At which the narrator comments: 'Then he collapsed over the parchments and died with his eyes open.' The massacre had been denied both by the locals and by the authorities: 'In Macondo nothing has happened, nor is anything happening now, nor will it ever' (p. 263). Then all history and all memory were comprehensively blotted out by the rain which lasted four years, eleven months and two days, and which recalls the previous 'plague of insomnia' in chapter 3, provoked on that occasion by the suppression of Indian history. Now proletarian history. was to be erased. In this instance, however, despite assiduous efforts by Colombia's official historians to make even the memory of the murdered strikers 'disappear', it was not to be so easy. The massacre was perpetrated by troops under General Carlos Cortés Vargas at the Ciénaga (Magdalena) railway station on 5 December 1928, in direct connivance with the

United Fruit Company. More than thirty thousand workers were on strike in the zone and it appears that at least four thousand were at the Ciénaga demonstration when the troops opened fire. The conservative government of Miguel Abadía Méndez (1926–30) reported that a mere nine strikers were killed and, like all succeeding regimes, set about suppressing the true story. After some tempestuous parliamentary debates in September 1929, almost nothing of importance concerning these events appeared in Colombia in the forty years up to the publication of *One Hundred Years of Solitude*.[27] The rest is silence.

After the interminable rain, Ursula's own 'one hundred torrential years' come to an end, and with it her morality and her view of the world, the cement that has held the family together until these final chapters. When she dies, Macondo's decline accelerates, and the doom of the entire Buendía family rapidly approaches. Nevertheless, as García Márquez reveals, all is not forgotten. First José Arcadio Segundo, then Aureliano Babilonia, keep the memory of the workers' struggles and their suppression alive, at the same time as they themselves strive to decipher the broader historical panorama encoded in the parchments in Melquíades's room. José Arcadio's first memory was of seeing a man executed by firing squad as a child, and as we decode his own life we perceive clearly that he is one of the few characters who has struggled in any way sincerely against injustice. He it is, then, who leads the strike; who begins to decipher the parchments, or 'true history', of the Buendía family; and who, as his legacy, educates young Aureliano Babilonia:

> In reality, although everyone took him for a madman, José Arcadio Segundo was at this time the most lucid member of the household. He taught little Aureliano to read and write, initiated him in the study of the parchments, and instilled in him so personal an interpretation of the meaning of the Banana Company for Macondo, that many years later, when Aureliano finally went out into the world, people would think that he was telling some hallucinatory story, because it was so radically opposed to the false version accepted by the historians and confirmed in the school textbooks. (p. 296)

Nothing, surely, could be clearer. After José Arcadio Segundo's death, Aureliano Babilonia remains in Melquiades's room, continuing his own education and the deciphering of the parchments, sometimes aided by the ghost of Melquiades himself. The room, needless to say, is that timeless space of memory, domain of history and literature (García Márquez in his writer's solitude), marked by 'the diaphanous purity of its air, its immunity against dust and destruction' (p. 264), until, that is, Melquiades himself dies and time pursues its work in his room also. Aureliano, meanwhile, obsessed by the parchments, takes no interest in what is going on around him and makes only occasional excursions to buy reference works at the old Catalan's bookshop (the political aftermath of the Spanish Civil War and its impact in Latin America). At length, having deduced that the manuscripts are written in Sanskrit, he manages to translate the first page, only to discover that they are poems and still in code. Finally, firmly 'fortified within written reality', he emerges into the real world and makes four new friends at the bookshop, thereafter dividing his time between books and brothels: 'Only then did it occur to him that literature was the best game ever devised for pulling the wool over people's eyes' (p. 327).

One of his new friends, Gabriel, is none other than the author, and his fiancée, Mercedes, is none other than the author's wife. Gabriel leaves for Europe to become a writer after winning a competition. This would be in 1954, in the midst of *la violencia*, when Colombia as a whole was indeed, like Macondo, in an advanced stage of social decomposition. It is to Gabriel that Aureliano, now left behind, had felt closest, for a very important reason. Both knew the story of the strike: 'Aureliano and Gabriel were linked by a sort of complicity, founded on real events in which no one else believed and which had so affected their lives that both were adrift in the wake of a world that was gone, and of which only their own nostalgic longings remained' (p. 329). Once again, could anything be clearer? García Márquez leaves the novel for Paris, but he also remains through the medium of Aureliano, who is so closely linked to him and to José Arcadio Segundo through their shared interpretation of the history of Macondo and of the Buendía family. Moreover, Aureliano is the character who eventually deciphers the parchments (the novel, his own life, Latin American history) on the very last page.

In that hypnotic final section we have the famous metaphor of dialectical decline, which is the Buendía family's historical spiral as understood by Pilar Ternera: '... the history of the family was a system of irreparable repetitions, a turning wheel which would have gone on spinning until eternity were it not for the progressive and irremediable wearing of the axle' (p. 334). Needless to say, the family members themselves had perceived no spiral, only cycles of futility: '"I know this off by heart", shrieked Ursula. "It's as though time were going round in circles and we'd come back to the beginning again"' (p. 169). 'Once more: she shivered at the realization that time did not pass, as she had just acknowledged, but merely went round and round in circles' (p. 284). Then, on the penultimate page, García Márquez explains not so much the nature of the family history as the inner theory of his novel: 'Melquíades had not arranged events in the order of man's conventional time, but had concentrated a whole century of daily episodes in such a way that they coexisted in a single instant' (p. 350). Again, the statement is not a philosophical speculation on the nature of time or the problems of literature, but a historical interpretation of reality in terms of what Cueva calls the 'great structural heterogeneity of Latin American social formations'.[28] This sudden focusing of the literary-structural problems involved in conveying uneven development through the classic bourgeois vehicle of the novel brings us at last to the central question of authorship and readership with which the novel ends.

It is the younger generation, that of García Márquez himself (Aureliano Babilonia and Gabriel), which finally comes to read and write the real history of the continent. They do so precisely by deciphering the magical reality and labyrinthine fantasies of the previous one hundred years of solitude, this very novel, which is their world, and in which so many other characters have been bewitched and bewildered. Hence the mirror/mirage (*espejos/espejismos*) ambiguity on the last page. There we find Aureliano Babilonia—and the author reminds us of his surname— 'deciphering the instant he was living, deciphering it as he lived it', or, as Zea would no doubt argue, negating the past dialectically in order to become, in Paz's phrase, 'contemporary with all men'. Thus he breaks out of false circularities, meaningless repetitions, the prehistory before the dawn of proletarian consciousness. Aureliano's reading literally puts an end to one hundred years of solitude, to *One Hundred Years of Solitude*, and turns the reader who is reading about him back out into the history outside the text.[29] The only remaining question is whether this is a logical outcome to the structural conception of the novel as a whole, or whether García Márquez has merely imposed it in a moment of inspiration, in order to escape, Houdini-like, from the implications of his own pessimistic philosophy. I think not, precisely because, as has been said, this is not so much a literary narration of Latin American history as a 'deconstructionist' reading of that history. Once the characters become able to interpret their own past, the author is able to end on an optimistic note. The apocalypse of the Buendías is not—how could it be?—the end of Latin America but the end of neocolonialism and its conscious or unconscious collaborators.

To those who complain that the novel does not *say* this, we can only ask: What other significance is there in the chain of memory from the Banana massacre through José Arcadio Segundo, Aureliano Babilonia, the fictional and the real Gabriel García Márquez, and the reader himself? Yet, if this reading is already Cervantine enough ('from Cide Hamete Benengeli to Melquíades the gypsy'), there is a further dimension to unfold. For the new novelists of the 1960s, the two key signs of the impending transformation of Latin America were the Cuban Revolution and the *boom* of the Latin American novel itself.[30] Cuba was perceived by Latin American socialists—and even, for a time, by liberals—as the material conversion of the workers' struggle into historical reality. Looking back from this vantage point, many years later, its seems obvious that the *boom*, which was announced by Julio Cortázar's *Rayuela* (*Hopscotch*) in 1963, reached its apotheosis with *One Hundred Years of Solitude* in 1967; and that the novel as text is perfectly aware of its own literary-historical significance, one whose implicit claim is that the *boom* itself is a proof of the end of neocolonialism and the beginning of true liberation. The celebrated 'inter-textual' references to Alejo Carpentier's *El siglo de las lutes* (*Explosion in a Cathedral*, 1962), Carlos Fuentes's *La muerte de Artemio Cruz* (*The Death of Artemio Cruz*, 1962), *Rayuela* itself and Mario Vargas Llosa's *La casa verde* (*The Green House*, 1966), are clear signs of this (as compared with, say Borges, whose textual references are overwhelmingly to literatures outside Latin America). The sense of euphoria in the novel, and particularly in its final pages—one can almost hear García Márquez shout *Eureka!*—is palpable. It communicates to us the excitement of a writer who has at long last solved his artistic problems by deciphering his own life history, who is aware that in the process he has written a classic, and, not only that, is also conscious that his work will appear at the perfect culminating moment in the political and literary history of his continent, encapsulating that history and his own biography at one and the same time.[31]

To this extent, one should perhaps revise the impression of a novel whose two levels, magical and realist, mythical and historical, are entirely inseparable, since after the massacre and the death of Ursula they slowly but surely begin to come apart. The opening of the novel— 'diaphanous', 'recent', bathed in light—is an evocation not only of Latin America's mythical innocence after Independence but of the magical childhood world García Márquez inhabited in Aracataca with his grandfather, the colonel.[32] The endless civil wars in the novel between liberals and conservatives bring no enlightenment, only disillusion and despair. Nevertheless, as the novel wears on and García Márquez himself as narrator gradually metamorphoses from child into adult (finally becoming fully himself only on the last page of the book), the characters slowly, reluctantly come to understand, among other things, what it is that Latin American colonels are generally paid to do, and innocence comes to an end. Whereas at the start of the text the characters are mainly optimistic and forward-looking, by the time the narrative is half-way through they begin to hear the music, not of hope and destiny, but of nostalgia for the past and for innocence itself. Once Ursula loses her residual faith in the purpose and coherence of the present, she dies, and once she has died the solid unity—or mystification—of myth and history is broken. The rest of the novel condenses the decipherment of Colombian history which García Márquez and his generation (especially the Grupo de Barranquilla) carried out in the wake of the 1948 *Bogotazo* (he was twenty years old at the time), when the workers' movement was again denied its place in national life, and on through the dark years of *la violencia*.[33] It seems clear that he was able to do this precisely by having distanced himself from these realities, escaping at last from Colombia, Aracataca, his family 'demons' (to quote Vargas Llosa). This is one more illustration of the truth that Latin American authors can best achieve greatness not through a national, still less a cosmopolitan, perspective but from a continental standpoint: by conceiving themselves as Latin Americans.

Seen in this multiple light, *One Hundred Years of Solitude* is clearly a demystification, though apparently one so labyrinthine in itself that most readers have managed to get themselves as lost in its winding corridors and spiralling stairways as most Latin Americans, including the Buendías, in the 'esperpentic'[34] history which it reconstructs.[35] My belief is that the major works of the boom were largely misread by critics, and that the writers themselves were misled by critical reaction to their texts into misinterpreting them, and thereafter—from about 1968—into giving the public what they mistakenly thought it wanted. No misreading could be more serious for Latin American literary history than the 'mythreading' of its most celebrated work, *One Hundred Years of Solitude*.

NOTES

1. L. Zea, *El pensamiento latinoamericano* (Mexico, 1965), p. 36, quotes Hegel's similar view: 'America is the land of the future ... It is a country longed for by those who are weary of Europe's historical museum'.

2. M. Deas, 'Politics and Violence: Aspects of *la violencia* in Colombia', *Encounter*, 25:3 (1965), 110–14. The article is invaluable for readers of *One Hundred Years of Solitude*.

3. García Márquez's stamp is already clearly visible in other 'Third World' novels, such as Salman Rushdie's *Midnight's Children*, whose ending is an evident salute to *One Hundred Years of Solitude*: 'because it is the privilege and the curse of midnight's children to be both masters and victims of their times, to forsake privacy and be sucked into the annihilating whirlpool of the multitudes, and to be unable to live or die in peace' (London, 1982, p. 463).

4. A. Dorfman, *Imaginación y violencia en América Latina* (2nd ed., Barcelona, 1972), sees in *One Hundred Years of Solitude* 'an immense expanse of time, in which the individual is swallowed up by history and history is swallowed up in turn by myth' (p. 152).

5. D.L. Shaw, 'Concerning the Interpretation of *Cien años de soledad*', *Ibero-Amerikanisches Archiv*, 3:4 (1977), 318–29 (p. 319).

6. *Ibid.*, p. 327.

7. In this sense *One Hundred Years of Solitude* reminds me of Carpentier's *Los pasos perdidos* (*The Lost Steps*, 1953), in which the author draws strength from his own weakness: the central theme becomes his own penchant for rhetoric which, as it immobilizes reality, reveals the inadequacy both of Latin American historiography and literary language

in their attempt to capture this new continent's reality. Likewise García Márquez is able to transfer to his characters his own weakness for hyperbole and fabulation, in order to subject it to a critique from the standpoint of his more conscious socialist perspective.

8. Part of the problem with García Márquez—ironically enough, in view of my interpretation of *One Hundred Years of Solitude*—is that he really does appear to have more difficulty than most men in telling literature from reality, fiction from truth. His journalism is full of what I would call *Blacamanismos*, and he can even turn a Salvador Allende into a potential character from one of his own novels: '... fate could only grant him that rare and tragic greatness of dying in armed defence of the anachronistic booby of bourgeois law' (*New Statesman*, 15 March 1974, p. 358).

9. A. Rama, 'Un novelista de la violencia americana', in P. S. Martínez (ed.), *Recopilación de textos sobre Gabriel García Márquez* (Havana, 1969), pp. 58–71 (p. 62).

10. J. Mejía Duque, *'El otoño del patriarca' o la crisis de la desmesura* (Bogota, 1975).

11. My initial impression of *Chronicle of a Death Foretold* (1981) is that we are back in the realm of *No One Writes to the Colonel*, although the pessimism is more pointed: the townsfolk themselves now share a collective guilt which used to be blamed on the 'outsiders'.

12. Rama, 'Un novelista', p. 63.

13. J. Ortega, *La contemplación y la fiesta* (Caracas, 1969), p. 125.

14. J.M. Oviedo, 'Macondo: un territorio mágico y americano', in *Nueve asedios a García Márquez* (3rd ed., Santiago de Chile, 1972), pp. 89–105 (p. 97).

15. E. Völkening, 'Anotado al margen de *Cien años de soledad*', in *Nueva novela latinoamericana*, ed. J. Lafforgue (Buenos Aires, 1969), vol. 1, p. 168.

16. Rama, 'Un novelista', p. 64.

17. I feel that Murena's neglected work, *El pecado original de América*, first published in 1954, has had an immense impact upon García Márquez's vision in *One Hundred Years of Solitude*. Even if this hypothesis is incorrect, a comparative study of the two texts would be illuminating. Another similarly suggestive work by García Márquez's compatriot, German Arciniegas, shows that cultural historians also can believe in their continent's magical reality: see the final chapter,

'Appointment with Necromancy', of his *Latin America: a Cultural History* (London, 1969).

18. A. Cueva, 'Para una interpretación sociológica de *Cien años de soledad*', *Revista Mexicana de Sociología*, 36 (1974), 59–76 (p. 67). No reader of *One Hundred Years of Solitude* can overlook this brilliant study.

19. T. Todorov, 'Macondo à Paris', in J. Leenhardt (ed.), *Littérature latino-américaine d'aujourd'hui* (Paris, 1980), pp. 316–34.

20. S. Benvenuto, 'Estética como historia', in *Recopilación de textos*, pp. 167–75 (p. 169).

21. One of the principal students of the phenomenon, E. Anderson Imbert, perceives the dangers of this confusion and then falls into the trap himself. See his *'El realismo mágico' y otros ensayos* (Caracas, 1976); also A. Flores, 'Magical Realism in Spanish American Fiction', *Hispania*, 38 (May 1955); and, above all, an invaluable recent study, J. Weisgerber, 'Le réalisme magique: la locution et le concept', *Revista di Letterature Moderne e Comparate*, 35:1 (1982), 27–53.

22. This, on the whole, is the view taken by Rama, Benvenuto and Cueva in the works already referred to, and by Jean Franco in various studies: significantly for literary history, it is also the view taken in the 1960s by Carlos Fuentes in his 'Macondo, sede del tiempo' (in *Recopilación*, pp. 119–22), and by Mario Vargas Llosa in his 'El Amadis en América' (*Recopilación*, pp. 113–18).

23. *One Hundred Years of Solitude*, p. 296. All references are to the 2nd edition, Buenos Aires, Sudamericana, 1968.

24. C. Blanco Aguinaga's excellent article on this topic, 'Realidad y estilo de Juan Rulfo', in J. Lafforgue (ed.), *Nueva novela latinoamericana* (Buenos Aires, 1969), pp. 85–113, is well known; it is all the more curious, then, that in his study 'Sobre la lluvia y la historia en las ficciones de García Márquez', in his *De mitólogos y novelistas* (Madrid, 1975), he completely misreads the conclusion of *One Hundred Years of Solitude*, failing to see that García Márquez has treated exactly the same phenomenon as Rulfo in almost exactly the same way. Juan Masoliver, 'Los cien engaños de García Márquez', *Bulletin of the Society for Latin American Studies*, 31 (October 1979), 22–37, takes a more judiciously critical but equally stringent view.

25. R. Gullón, *García Márquez o el olvidado arte de contar* (Madrid, 1970).

26. M. Vargas Llosa, *García Márquez: historia de un deicidio*

(Barcelona, Barral, 1971). This remains the fundamental source work on García Márquez.

27. A recent documentary anthology, *1928: La masacre en las Bananeras* (Bogotá, n.d.), reprints the parliamentary debates of 1929, and in particular the protests of two politicians, Jorge Eliécer Gaitán and Gabriel Turbay, together with a number of eye-witness accounts, including the vital contribution of none other than the parish priest of Aracataca, Father Francisco Angarita (in a letter dated 16 July 1929). In the introduction the editors claim, like García Márquez in his novel, that 'the official version of Colombian history has tried by every means to omit or distort this bloody episode' (p. 5). Turbay himself had underlined the policy of censorship in a speech on 3 September 1929 when he referred to the 'tragic and horrifying secret of the endless chain of ignominious acts committed during the apocalyptic march of the military through the banana zone'. Fifty years later H. Rodríguez Acosta, in his *Elementos críticos para una nueva interpretación de la historia colombiana* (Bogotá, 1979), would still be making the same point: 'This episode of Colombian history has been repeatedly ignored by our historians because to reveal it would damage the reputation of the ruling class' (p. 203).

28. Cueva, 'Para una interpretación sociológica', p. 59. Cueva's brilliant study fails, in my opinion, to recognize that García Márquez's critique of imperialism is always far more radical than his critique of capitalism itself. This is a feature of the entire *nueva novela* as a historical phenomenon.

29. G. Brotherston indicates this effect in *The Emergence of the Latin American Novel* (Cambridge, 1977), noting that it '"opens" the novel to include and involve the reader, as Umberto Eco has defined that process' (p. 135).

30. Thus Mario Vargas Llosa: 'This seems to me a symptom, the sign of great historical changes to come in Latin America ... All the great eras of the novel have taken place just before some social apocalypse', quoted in H. Cattolica, 'Vargas Llosa: Europa y el escritor latinoamericano', *El Escarabajo de Oro*, 33 (March 1967), 20–32.

31. In this regard one could draw illuminating comparisons between *Cien años de soledad* and Asturias's *Hombres de maíz*. See my critical edition of the latter, *Hombres de maíz* (Edición Crítica de las Obras Completas de Miguel Angel Asturias, vol. 4, Klincksieck, Paris, and Fondo de

Cultura Económica, Mexico, 1981). *One Hundred Years of Solitude* in fact appeared in the year in which Asturias was awarded the Nobel Prize. The two writers, who probably had more in common with one another than with any other Latin American authors except perhaps Rulfo and Guimarães Rosa, evidently recognized their implicit filiation and engaged in a brief and rather vulgar polemic which did neither much credit. Asturias, belatedly crowned, feared the young pretender, and García Márquez, newly acclaimed, was bent on parricide. (Specifically, he vowed that with his new project *El otoño del patriarca*, he would 'teach' the author of *El señor Presidente* 'how to write a real dictator novel'.)

32. M. Vargas Llosa, 'García Márquez: de Aracataca a Macondo', in *Nueve asedios*, pp. 126–46: 'Aracataca was living on its memories when he was born: his fictions, in turn, would live off his memories of Aracataca' (p. 128).

33. This historical thread in fact coincides with that of the life and death of Jorge Eliécer Gaitán, who in 1929 was the principal critic of the government's role in the Banana massacres ('We know to our sorrow that in this country the government points its murderous machine guns at the fatherland's own sons and its trembling knees to the ground in the face of yankee gold'), and whose assassination, as presidential candidate for the Liberal party, led to the 1948 *Bogotazo* and the horrific period of general violence that followed over the next two decades, of which García Márquez's novels *No One Writes to the Colonel* (1958) and *In Evil Hour* (1962) show only the blood-chilling icy tip.

34. Valle-Inclán's term for his grotesque and distorting dramatic vision of Spanish history.

35. There are many novels in Latin America after 1945 about characters whose quests—whether conscious or unconscious—show the reader the way out of the historical labyrinth and at the same time flatter him, to quote Borges on Herbert Quain, that he is 'more perspicacious than the detective'. Examples are Asturias's *Hombres de maíz* (*Men of Maize*, 1949), Marechal's *Adán Buenosayres* (*Adam Buenosaires*, 1948), Carpentier's *Los pasos perdidos* (*The Lost Steps*, 1953), Rulfo's *Pedro Páramo* (1955), Fuentes's *La muerte de Artemio Cruz* (*The Death of Artemio Cruz*, 1962), Cortázar's *Rayuela* (*Hopscotch*, 1963), José Lezama Lima's *Paradiso* (1966), and Vargas Llosa's *La casa verde* (*The Green House*, 1966), all of them Modernist, 'Ulyssean' works completed before the onset of 'Post-Modernism' in the Latin American 1970s. For further consideration of

these issues, see my '"Boom", Yes; "New" Novel, No: Further Reflections on the Optical Illusions of the 1960s in Latin America', *Bulletin of Latin American Research*, 3:2 (1984), 53–63; 'The Literature, Music and Art of Latin America from 1870 to 1930', *Cambridge History of Latin America*, vol. 4 (1986), pp. 443–526; and *James Joyce and Latin American Fiction* (University of Calgary Press, 1987).

Chronology

1928	Gabriel José García Márquez is born on March 6 in Aracataca, Colombia to Gabriel Eligio García and Luisa Santiaga Márquez Iguarán. Spends the first eight years of his childhood with his maternal grandparents.
1936–1940	When he is eight years old, his grandfather dies, and he goes to live with his parents in Sucre. He is sent to boarding school in Barranquilla.
1940	Wins a scholarship to the Liceo Nacional de Zipaquirá, near Bogotá.
1947	Enters the Universidad Nacional in Bogotá to study law. Publishes his first short story "La tercera resignación" ("The Third Resignation") in *El Espectador*, a Bogotá newspaper.
1948	Liberal Presidential candidate Jorge Eliécer Gaintán is assassinated; civil war erupts in Columbia, known as *la violencia*. García Márquez moves to Cartagena on the coast. Continues law studies and writes a column for the newspaper, *El Universal*.
1950	Quits law school. Moves to Barranquilla and writes a column for the newspaper *El Heraldo*.
1953	Quits journalism temporarily and travels around Colombia working various jobs.
1954	Returns to Bogotá. Writes articles and film reviews for *El Espectador.*

1955	Wins a national prize for a short story, and publishes his first novel, *La hojarasca* (*Leaf Storm*). Writes account of Luis Alejandro Velasco's survival at sea for *El Espectador*. Travels to Geneva as a correspondent. The government closes down *El Espectador* and García Márquez stays in Europe.
1956	Lives in Paris and works on manuscripts for two novels, *La mala hora* (*In Evil Hour*) and *El coronel no tiene quien la escriba* (*No One Writes to the Colonel*).
1957	Finishes *No One Writes to the Colonel*. Travels to East Germany, Czechoslovakia, Poland, Russia, and Hungary. Moves to Caracas to work for the newspaper *Momento*.
1958	Marries Mercedes Barcha. Writes almost all of the stories in the collection *Los funerales de la Mama Grande* (*Big Mama's Funeral*).
1959–61	Cuban Revolution. Works for Cuba's Prensa Latina in Bogotá, Cuba, and New York. His first child, Rodrigo, is born.
1961	Resigns from Prensa Latina. Makes "Homage to Faulkner" bus trip across the Deep South to Mexico City, where he is an editor for magazines. Awarded the Colombian Esso Literary Prize for *In Evil Hour*.
1962	Publishes *Big Mama's Funeral* and *No One Writes to the Colonel*. A censored *In Evil Hour* is published in Spain. His second son, Gonzalo, is born.
1963	Works for advertising agency and writes films.
1965	Goes into seclusion to write *Cien años de soledad* (*One Hundred Years of Solitude*).
1966	Authorized version of *In Evil Hour* is published in Mexico.
1967	*One Hundred Years of Solitude* is published in Buenos Aires. Moves to Barcelona, Spain.
1968	*No One Writes to the Colonel* published in the United States.
1969	*One Hundred Years of Solitude* wins the Chianchiano Prize in Italy and is named the Best Foreign Book in France.

1970	*One Hundred Years of Solitude* is published in English and chosen as one of twelve best books of the year by U.S. critics.
1971	Peruvian novelist Mario Vargas Llosa publishes the first book-length study of García Márquez's life and work, *Gabriel García Márquez: Historia de un deicidio.* García Márquez receives an honorary Doctorate of Letters from Columbia University.
1972	Awarded Rómulo Gallegos Prize. Publishes *La increíble y triste de la cándida Eréndira y de su abuela desalmada (The Incredible and Sad Tale of Innocent Eréndira and her Heartless Grandmother).* Awarded *Books Abroad/* Neustadt Prize. *Leaf Storm and Other Stories* published in New York.
1974	Founds *Alternativa*, a leftist magazine, in Bogotá.
1975	Publishes *El otoño del patriarca (The Autumn of the Patriarch).* Leaves Spain and returns to Mexico.
1976	*The Autumn of the Patriarch* is published in New York.
1977	Publishes *Operación Carlota (Operation Carlota)*, essays on Cuba's role in Africa.
1978	*Innocent Eréndira and Other Stories* published in the United States.
1979	English translation of *In Evil Hour* published in the United States.
1981	Publishes *Crónica de una muerta anunciada (Chronicle of a Death Foretold).* Awarded the French Legion of Honor Medal. When he returns to Colombia from Cuba, the government accuses him of financing a guerrilla group, and he flees and seeks political asylum in Mexico.
1981	*Obra periodística*, four volumes of his journalistic pieces, edited by Jacques Gilard, is published.
1982	Awarded Nobel Prize for Literature. Publishes *El olor de la guayaba (The Fragrance of Guava)*, conversations with Plinio Apuleyo Mendoza. Writes *Viva Sandino*, a screenplay about the Nicaraguan revolution.

1983	Returns to Colombia from his exile in Mexico. *Chronicle of a Death Foretold* published in the United States.
1984	*Collected Stories* is published in the United States.
1985	Publishes *El amor en los tiempos del cólera* (*Love in the Time of Cholera*), a novel. The English translation is released in the United States in 1988.
1986	*La adventura de Miguel Littín, clandestino en Chile*, a work of nonfiction, published. *The Story of a Shipwrecked Sailor*, his tale of Luis Alejandro Velasco's survival, published in the United States.
1987	*Clandestine in Chile: The Adventures of Miguel Littín* published in the United States.
1989	The novel *El general en su labertino* (*The General in His Labyrinth*) is published in Argentina, Colombia, Mexico and Spain. A year later the English translation is published in the United States.
1992	*Doce cuentos peregrinos* (*Strange Pilgrims: Twelve Stories*) published Madrid. A year later, English translation published in the United States.
1994	*Del amor y otros demonios* (*Of Love and Other Demons*) published in Barcelona. A year later, the English translation published in the United States.
1996	*Noticia de un secuestro* (*News of Kidnapping*) published. A year later, the English translation is published.
1998	He is a guest of Fidel Castro's during the historic visit of Pope John Paul II to Colombia.
1999	Purchases *Cambio*, a Colombian newsmagazine. In June he is hospitalized for fatigue; in September he goes to Los Angeles to undergo treatment for lymphatic cancer.
2001	Publishes first volume of memoirs, called *Vivir para contarla* (*Living to Tell the Tale*).
2003	*Living to Tell the Tale* is published in the United States.
2004	Publishes *Memoria de mis putas tristes*.

Works by Gabriel García Marquez

La hojarasca, 1955.

El coronel no tiene quien le escriba, 1961.

Los funerales de la Mamá Grande, 1962.

La mala hora, 1962.

Cien años de soledad, 1967.

Isabel viendo llover en Macondo, 1967.

Ojos de perro azul, 1972.

La increíble y triste historia de la cándida Eréndira y de su abuela desalmada, 1972.

Cuando era feliz e indocumentado, 1974.

*Cuatro cuentos,*1974.

El otoño del patriarca, 1975.

Todos los cuentos de Gabriel García Márquez (1947–1972), 1975.

Crónicas y reportajes, 1976.

Operación Carlota, 1977.

Periodismo militante, 1978.

Crónica de una muerte anunciada, 1981.

Obra periodística, 1981.

El amor en los tiempos del cólera, 1985.

La adventura de Miguel Littín, clandestino en Chile, 1986.

El general en su labertino, 1989.

Doce cuentos peregrinos, 1992.

Del amor y otros demonios, 1994.

Noticia de un secuestro, 1996.

Vivir para contarla, 2001.

Memoria de mis putas tristes, 2004.

PRINCIPAL TRANSLATIONS IN ENGLISH

No One Writes to the Colonel and Other Stories. Trans. J.S. Bernstein, 1968.

One Hundred Years of Solitude. Trans. Gregory Rabassa, 1970.

Leaf Storm and Other Stories. Trans. Gregory Rabassa, 1972.

The Autumn of the Patriarch. Trans. Gregory Rabassa, 1976.

Innocent Eréndira and Other Stories. Trans. Gregory Rabassa, 1978.

In Evil Hour. Trans. Gregory Rabassa, 1979.

Chronicle of a Death Foretold. Trans. Gregory Rabassa, 1983.

The Fragrance of Guava: Plinio Apuleyo Mendoza in Conversation with Gabriel

García Márquez, Trans. Ann Wright, 1983.

Collected Stories, 1984.

The Story of a Shipwrecked Sailor. Trans. Randolph Hogan, 1986.

Clandestine in Chile: The Adventures of Miguel Littín. Trans. Asa Zatz, 1987.

Love in the Time of Cholera. Trans. Edith Grossman, 1988.

The General in His Labyrinth. Trans. Edith Grossman, 1990.

Strange Pilgrims: Twelve Stories, Trans. Edith Grossman, 1993.

Of Love and Other Demons, Trans. Edith Grossman, 1995

News of Kidnapping, Trans. Edith Grossman, 1997.

Collected Novellas, Trans. Gregory Rabassa and J.S. Bernstein, 1999.

Living to Tell the Tale, Trans. Edith Grossman, 2003.

Works about Gabriel García Márquez

Adams, Robert M. "Big Little Book." *The New York Review of Books*, 14 April 1983: 3.

Alèthea 13 (Spring-Summer 1984). Gabriel *García Márquez: The Man and the Magic of His Writings*. Ed. Ricardo Pastor.

Bell, Michael. *Gabriel García Márquez: Solitude and Solidarity*. New York: St. Martin's Press, 1993.

Bell-Villada, Gene H. *García Márquez: The Man and His Work*. Chapel Hill: The University of North Carolina Press, 1990.

———. "Pronoun Shifters, Virginia Woolf, Bela Bartók, Plebeian Forms, Real-Life Tyrants, and the Shaping of García Márquez's *Patriarch*." *Contemporary Literature* 28, no. 4 (Winter 1987–88): 460–82.

———. "Names and Narrative Pattern in *One Hundred Years of Solitude*." *Latin American Literary Review* 9, no. 18 (1981): 37–46.

Bloom, Harold, ed. *Modern Critical Views: Gabriel García Márquez*. New York: Chelsea House Publishers, 1989.

Brushwood, John. S. "Reality and Imagination in the Novels of García Márquez." *Latin American Literary Review* 25 (1985): 9–14.

Davis, Mary E. "The Town That Was an Open Wound." *Comparative Literature Studies* 23, no. 1 (Spring 1986): 24–43.

Dolan, Sean. *Gabriel García Márquez*. New York: Chelsea House, 1994.

Donoso, José. *The Boom in Spanish American Literature*. Trans. Gregory Kolvakos. NY: Columbia University Press, 1977.

Dreifus, Claudia. "Playboy Interview: Gabriel García Márquez." *Playboy* 30, no. 3, February 1983: 65+.

Duran, Armando. "Conversation with Gabriel García Márquez." *Review* 70 (1971): 109–18.

Earle, Pete G., ed. *Gabriel García Márquez*. Madrid: Taurus, 1981.

Fau, Margaret Eustella. *Gabriel García Márquez: An Annotated Bibliography, 1947–1979*. Westport, CT: Greenwood Press, 1980.

————, and Nelly Sefir de González. *Bibliographic Guide to Gabriel García Márquez, 1979–1985*. Westport, CT: Greenwood Press, 1986.

Fuentes, Carlos. "Gabriel García Márquez: la segunda lectura," in *La nueva novela hispanoamericana*. Mexico City: Joaquín Mortiz, 1969: 58–67.

————. *Gabriel García Márquez and the Invention of America*. Liverpool, England: Liverpool University Press, 1987.

Gallagher, D.P. "Gabriel García Márquez," in *Modern Latin American Literature*. London: Oxford University Press, 1973.

Guibert, Rita. "Gabriel García Márquez," in *Seven Voices: Seven Latin American Writers Talk to Rita Guibert*. New York: Knopf, 1973. 305–37.

Janes, Regina. *Gabriel García Márquez: Revolution in Wonderland*. Columbia: University of Missouri Press, 1981.

Kakutani, Michiko. "García Márquez Novel Covers Love and Time." *The New York Times*, 6 April 1988, C21.

Latin American Literary Review 13 (Jan–June 1985). *Special Issue: Gabriel García Márquez*. Eds. Yvette E. Miller and Charles Rossman.

McGuirk, Bernard and Richard Cardwell, eds. *Gabriel García Márquez: New Readings*. New York: Cambridge University Press, 1987.

McMurray, George R. *Gabriel García Márquez*. New York: Ungar, 1977.

McNerney, Kathleen. *Understanding Gabriel García Márquez*. South Carolina: University of South Carolina, 1989.

Mellen, Joan. *Gabriel García Márquez: Literary Masters, vol. 5*. Detroit: The Gale Group, 2000.

Minta, Stephen. *Gabriel García Márquez: Writer of Colombia*. London: Jonathan Cape, 1987.

Oberhelman, Harley D. *The Presence of Faulkner in the Writings of García Márquez*. Lubbock: Texas Tech Press, 1980.

Rodman, Selden. "Gabriel García Márquez," in *Tongues of Fallen Angels: Conversations*. New York: New Directions, 1974.

Rodriguez Monegal, Emir. "*One Hundred Years of Solitude*: The Last Three Pages." *Books Abroad 47* (1973): 485–89.

Shaw, Bradley A. and Nora Vera-Goodwin, eds. *Critical Perspectives on Gabriel García Márquez*. Lincoln, Nebraska: Society of Spanish and Spanish-American Studies, 1986.

Sims, Robert L. "The Banana Massacre in *Cien años de soledad*: A Micro-Structural Example of Myth, History, and Bricolage." *Chasqui 8*, no. 3 (1979): 3–23.

———. *The Evolution of Myth in Gabriel García Márquez from* La Hojarasca *to* Cien años de soledad. Miami, FL: Ediciones Universal, 1981.

Stone, Peter. "Gabriel García Márquez" in *Writers At Work: The Paris Review Interviews—Sixth Series*. George Plimpton, ed. New York: Viking, 1984. 313–339.

Vargas Llosa, Mario. *Gabriel García Márquez: historia de un deicidio*. Barcelona: Barral Editores, 1971.

Williams, Raymond. *Gabriel García Márquez*. Boston: Twayne, 1984.

Wood, Michael. *Gabriel García Márquez: One Hundred Years of Solitude*. Cambridge & New York: Cambridge University Press, 1990.

WEBSITES:

Gabriel García Marquez: Macondo—Author Home Page
www.themodernword.com/gabo/

Gabriel García Márquez
www.kirjasto.sci.fi/marquez.htm

Literature 1982 (Nobel Prize)
http://nobelprize.org/literature/laureates/1982/

The Nobel Prize Internet Archive
www.almaz.com/nobel/literature/1982a.html

Contributors

HAROLD BLOOM is Sterling Professor of the Humanities at Yale University. He is the author of over 20 books, including *Shelley's Mythmaking* (1959), *The Visionary Company* (1961), *Blake's Apocalypse* (1963), *Yeats* (1970), *A Map of Misreading* (1975), *Kabbalah and Criticism* (1975), *Agon: Toward a Theory of Revisionism* (1982), *The American Religion* (1992), *The Western Canon* (1994), and *Omens of Millennium: The Gnosis of Angels, Dreams, and Resurrection* (1996). *The Anxiety of Influence* (1973) sets forth Professor Bloom's provocative theory of the literary relationships between the great writers and their predecessors. His most recent books include *Shakespeare: The Invention of the Human* (1998), a 1998 National Book Award finalist, *How to Read and Why* (2000), *Genius: A Mosaic of One Hundred Exemplary Creative Minds* (2002), *Hamlet: Poem Unlimited* (2003), and *Where Shall Wisdom be Found* (2004). In 1999, Professor Bloom received the prestigious American Academy of Arts and Letters Gold Medal for Criticism, and in 2002 he received the Catalonia International Prize.

AMY SICKELS is a freelance writer living in New York City. She received her MFA in creative writing from Penn State University and she has published short stories, essays, and book reviews in numerous journals, including *Fourth Genre*, *Kalliope*, and *Literary Review*.

GRACE KIM's essay "Then They All Move On Again: Knowledge and the Individual in Judge Holden's Doctrine of War" on Cormac

McCarthy's novel *Blood Meridian* appeared in *Cormac McCarthy* as part of the Modern Critical Views series published by Chelsea House Publishers and her essay "The Human Drama in the Work of William Shakespeare" appeared in the Bloom's BioCritique volume on William Shakespeare.

GABRIEL GARCÍA MÁRQUEZ is an acclaimed author and journalist and winner of the 1982 Nobel Prize for Literature. Ever since the publication of *La hojarasca* (*Leaf Storm*) García Márquez has been considered a pioneering voice in Latin American writing.

GERALD MARTIN is a Professor in Hispanic Languages and Literature at the University of Pittsburgh. His publications include critical editions of Asturias's *Hombres de Maiz* (1981) and *El Señor Presidente* (2000); *Journeys through the Labyrinth: Latin American Fiction in the Twentieth Century* (1989); along with several major essays on Latin American cultural history in the *Cambridge History of Latin America* (1985–1995).

INDEX

121